# TASTING NOTES

COMPILED BY

D1363862

# INTRODUCTION

You might be tasting your whiskey wrong. We don't mean to suggest that you are actually putting it in your mouth improperly or that your taste buds are faulty. We're arguing that your deeper purpose may be misdirected, and therefore your method is perhaps flawed.

We are taught that tasting whiskey is a search for greatness, for that one, singular, perfect, platonic ideal, so you can forevermore say, "Give me the best, and damn the rest." But this attitude will lead you in the wrong direction, often toward expensive and obscure bottles, without much gratification.

We drink in a great time, when price and quality often have no correlation. We also drink in an era of multiplicity. Craft distillers and established whiskey makers alike are offering unusual and creative spirits that defy convention. And yet the pursuit of a vague notion of perfection remains the prevailing attitude in whiskey tasting.

Contrast this with the way people order beer. Nobody slams their fist down on a bar and yells, "Give me the absolute best," and then demands an obscure brew (while making very sure that everyone in proximity can hear and appreciate their good taste). People ordering beer favor variety, local interest, and peculiarity. People find styles they like and develop loyalties, but they also strike out and try new things. Multiplicity is part of beer culture and should be a part of whiskey culture, too.

So use this journal as a guide, not to find the perfect whiskey but to explore the breadth of whiskies. Sure, you'll find some you like and some you don't, but if there's anything that the long history of whiskey tells us, it's that what is considered great today will be tomorrow's swill. Nothing follows a fad like liquor.

But this, too, is liberating once you acknowledge it. The project is to get to know your whiskies and compare your taste over time. Taste them blind whenever possible (i.e., fill out the bottom of a tasting page first). Age and provenance are rarely the purported measure of excellence; better not to know, and let yourself be surprised by your own insights.

The guided tasting pages in this journal include some of the basic factors that we take into account when we taste whiskey. The focus of the pages is on utility. Not that you want to drink whiskey with a pen in hand, but sometimes being rigorous helps enhance an experience. And drinking whiskey is, after all, one of the most rewarding pursuits life offers, so you might as well jump in with conviction. Good luck.

COLIN SPOELMAN AND DAVID HASKELL
Co-founders, Kings County Distillery

# WHAT AM I DRINKING?

The landscape of distilled spirits can be very confusing, but every liquor can be classified based on four major variables: how it is aged, how it is distilled, what it is made from, and where it is made. Unaged spirits are clear and aged spirits are yellow to brown. Darker spirits are usually aged in new barrels, from which they absorb more flavor, and lighter spirits are usually aged in used barrels. In general, more flavorful spirits are distilled in pot stills to a low proof, and more neutral spirits are distilled in column stills to a higher proof. Grain, fruit, sugar, and agave are the most common ingredients. And because countries have often protected the types of spirits they produce, geography plays a role in what spirits may be called.

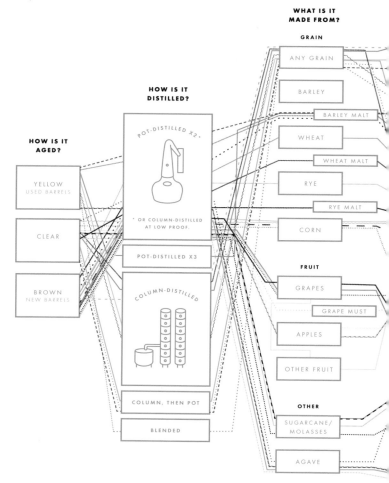

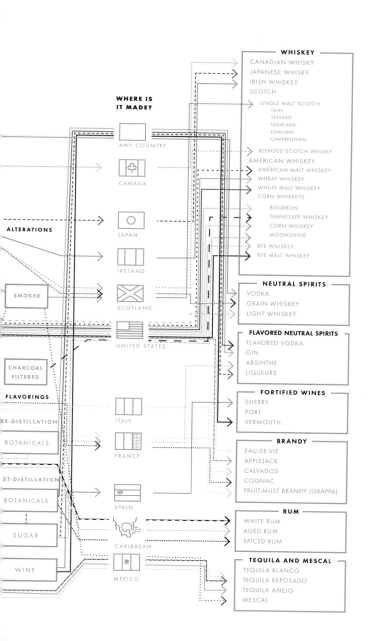

WHERE IS
IT MADE?

ANY COUNTRY

CANADA

JAPAN

IRELAND

SCOTLAND

UNITED STATES

ITALY

FRANCE

SPAIN

CARIBBEAN

MEXICO

ALTERATIONS

SMOKED

CHARCOAL
FILTERED

FLAVORINGS

RE-DISTILLATION

BOTANICALS

ST-DISTILLATION

BOTANICALS

SUGAR

WINE

WHISKEY
CANADIAN WHISKY
JAPANESE WHISKY
IRISH WHISKEY
SCOTCH
SINGLE MALT SCOTCH
ISLAY
SPEYSIDE
HIGHLAND
LOWLAND
CAMPBELTOWN
BLENDED SCOTCH WHISKY
AMERICAN WHISKEY
AMERICAN MALT WHISKEY
WHEAT WHISKEY
WHEAT MALT WHISKEY
CORN WHISKEYS
BOURBON
TENNESSEE WHISKEY
CORN WHISKEY
MOONSHINE
RYE WHISKEY
RYE MALT WHISKEY

NEUTRAL SPIRITS
VODKA
GRAIN WHISKEY
LIGHT WHISKEY

FLAVORED NEUTRAL SPIRITS
FLAVORED VODKA
GIN
ABSINTHE
LIQUEURS

FORTIFIED WINES
SHERRY
PORT
VERMOUTH

BRANDY
EAU-DE-VIE
APPLEJACK
CALVADOS
COGNAC
FRUIT-MUST BRANDY (GRAPPA)

RUM
WHITE RUM
AGED RUM
SPICED RUM

TEQUILA AND MESCAL
TEQUILA BLANCO
TEQUILA REPOSADO
TEQUILA AÑEJO
MESCAL

# WHISKEY BRANDS

Here is a selection of whiskies to help start your own tasting process. It's not intended to be comprehensive or used as a list of must-tries. Some of these whiskeys, especially those from Japan, are hard to find. Generally excluded are the so-called non-distiller-produced (NDP) whiskeys (bottlers who buy whiskey in bulk from other distilleries and package it as their own), although a few are included if the maker does something interesting with the product (Angel's Envy, for instance).

## AMERICAN WHISKEYS
### › BOURBON

#### › Traditional Mash Bill Bourbon
- [ ] BAKER'S
- [ ] BLACK MAPLE HILL
- [ ] BOOKER'S
- [ ] BUFFALO TRACE
- [ ] EAGLE RARE
- [ ] ELIJAH CRAIG
- [ ] ELMER T. LEE
- [ ] EVAN WILLIAMS
- [ ] EZRA BROOKS
- [ ] GEORGE T. STAGG
- [ ] HEAVEN HILL
- [ ] JIM BEAM
- [ ] KNOB CREEK
- [ ] NOAH'S MILL
- [ ] OLD CHARTER
- [ ] OLD FORESTER
- [ ] OLD TAYLOR
- [ ] PURE KENTUCKY
- [ ] ROWAN'S CREEK
- [ ] WATHEN'S
- [ ] WILD TURKEY
- [ ] WOODFORD RESERVE

#### › High Rye Bourbon
- [ ] ANCIENT AGE
- [ ] BASIL HAYDEN'S
- [ ] BLANTON'S
- [ ] BRECKENRIDGE
- [ ] BULLEIT
- [ ] BULLEIT 10
- [ ] FOUR ROSES SINGLE BARREL
- [ ] FOUR ROSES YELLOW LABEL
- [ ] OLD GRAND-DAD

#### › Wheated Bourbon
- [ ] LARCENY
- [ ] MAKER'S 46
- [ ] MAKER'S MARK
- [ ] OLD FITZGERALD
- [ ] OLD RIP VAN WINKLE
- [ ] PAPPY VAN WINKLE
- [ ] REBEL YELL
- [ ] W. L. WELLER

#### › Tennessee Whiskey*
- [ ] COLLIER AND MCKEEL
- [ ] GENTLEMAN JACK
- [ ] GEORGE DICKEL NO. 8
- [ ] GEORGE DICKEL NO. 12
- [ ] JACK DANIEL'S
- [ ] PRICHARD'S

#### › Other Bourbons
- [ ] BERKSHIRE
- [ ] GARRISON BROTHERS TEXAS
- [ ] HUDSON BABY
- [ ] HUDSON FOUR GRAIN
- [ ] KINGS COUNTY
- [ ] KOVAL SINGLE BARREL
- [ ] SMOOTH AMBLER YEARLING
- [ ] TOWN BRANCH
- [ ] WOODINVILLE WHISKEY CO.

### › RYE WHISKEY
- [ ] BULLEIT
- [ ] COPPER FOX
- [ ] CORSAIR RYEMAGEDDON
- [ ] DAD'S HAT
- [ ] FLEISCHMANN'S
- [ ] JIM BEAM
- [ ] OLD OVERHOLT
- [ ] OLD POTRERO
- [ ] PIKESVILLE
- [ ] RITTENHOUSE

- [ ] SAZERAC
- [ ] THOMAS H. HANDY SAZERAC
- [ ] WILD TURKEY
- [ ] WILLETT FAMILY ESTATE

### › WHITE WHISKEY
- [ ] BUFFALO TRACE WHITE DOG MASH #1
- [ ] COPPER RUN OZARK MOUNTAIN MOONSHINE
- [ ] CORSAIR WRY MOON
- [ ] GEORGIA MOON
- [ ] HIGH WEST SILVER WHISKEY— WESTERN OAT
- [ ] HUDSON NEW YORK CORN WHISKEY
- [ ] JACK DANIEL'S UNAGED TENNESSEE RYE
- [ ] JIM BEAM JACOB'S GHOST
- [ ] KINGS COUNTY MOONSHINE
- [ ] KOVAL
- [ ] LOW GAP
- [ ] OLE SMOKY MOONSHINE
- [ ] TROY AND SONS PLATINUM
- [ ] VIRGINIA LIGHTNING

### › MALT WHISKEY
- [ ] BALCONES TEXAS SINGLE MALT
- [ ] CORSAIR TRIPLE SMOKE
- [ ] LOST SPIRITS LEVIATHAN II
- [ ] MCCARTHY'S OREGON SINGLE MALT
- [ ] NEW HOLLAND ZEPPELIN BEND
- [ ] PEARSE LYONS RESERVE
- [ ] ST. GEORGE SINGLE MALT
- [ ] STRANAHAN'S
- [ ] WASMUND'S SINGLE MALT
- [ ] WESTLAND AMERICAN SINGLE MALT

> OTHER AMERICAN WHISKEYS

- [ ] ANGEL'S ENVY
- [ ] BALCONES TRUE BLUE
- [ ] BERNHEIM
- [ ] DRY FLY WASHINGTON WHEAT
- [ ] EARLY TIMES
- [ ] HIGH WEST BOURYE
- [ ] HIGH WEST CAMPFIRE
- [ ] KENTUCKY GENTLEMAN
- [ ] KOVAL SINGLE BARREL OAT
- [ ] MELLOW CORN

## SCOTCH WHISKIES
> SINGLE MALT SCOTCH

- [ ] ARDBEG
- [ ] AUCHENTOSHAN
- [ ] BALVENIE
- [ ] BOWMORE
- [ ] BRUICHLADDICH
- [ ] CAOL ILA
- [ ] DALWHINNIE
- [ ] GLENFARCLAS
- [ ] GLENFIDDICH
- [ ] GLENMORANGIE
- [ ] GLENROTHES
- [ ] HIGHLAND PARK
- [ ] LAGAVULIN
- [ ] LAPHROAIG
- [ ] LEDAIG
- [ ] THE MACALLAN
- [ ] OBAN
- [ ] STRATHISLA
- [ ] TALISKER

> BLENDED MALT WHISKY

- [ ] COMPASS BOX PEAT MONSTER
- [ ] COMPASS BOX SPICE TREE
- [ ] JOHNNIE WALKER GREEN LABEL

> BLENDED GRAIN WHISKY

- [ ] COMPASS BOX HEDONISM

> BLENDED SCOTCH WHISKY

- [ ] BALLANTINE'S
- [ ] CHIVAS REGAL
- [ ] CUTTY SARK
- [ ] DEWAR'S
- [ ] THE FAMOUS GROUSE
- [ ] J&B
- [ ] JOHNNIE WALKER BLACK LABEL
- [ ] JOHNNIE WALKER RED LABEL

## IRISH WHISKEYS

- [ ] BUSHMILLS
- [ ] CONNEMARA
- [ ] GREEN SPOT
- [ ] JAMESON
- [ ] KILBEGGAN
- [ ] MIDLETON
- [ ] PADDY
- [ ] POWERS
- [ ] REDBREAST
- [ ] TULLAMORE DEW
- [ ] TYRCONNELL

## CANADIAN WHISKIES

- [ ] ALBERTA PREMIUM
- [ ] CANADIAN CLUB
- [ ] CANADIAN MIST
- [ ] COLLINGWOOD
- [ ] CROWN ROYAL
- [ ] FORTY CREEK
- [ ] GLEN BRETON RARE
- [ ] LORD CALVERT
- [ ] PENDLETON
- [ ] SEAGRAM'S

## JAPANESE WHISKIES

- [ ] HAKUSHU SINGLE MALT
- [ ] HIBIKI
- [ ] ICHIRO'S MALT CHICHIBU
- [ ] NIKKA COFFEY GRAIN WHISKEY
- [ ] NIKKA MIYAGIKYO
- [ ] NIKKA TAKETSURU PURE MALT
- [ ] YAMAZAKI SINGLE MALT
- [ ] YOICHI SINGLE MALT

## INTERNATIONAL WHISKIES

- [ ] THE BELGIAN OWL (BELGIUM)
- [ ] BRENNE (FRANCE)
- [ ] KAVALAN (TAIWAN)
- [ ] MACKMYRA (SWEDEN)
- [ ] PENDERYN (WALES)

---

*Tennessee whiskey has never been well defined by law. State laws passed in 2013 defined Tennessee whiskey as bourbon made in Tennessee filtered through charcoal before barreling. There is a pending initiative to further refine (and partially relax) what can be called Tennessee whiskey. So the category is in flux, but most feel comfortable calling it a subtype of bourbon.

# TASTING NOTES

| DATE | |
|---|---|
| LOCATION | |

**WHISKEY**

DISTILLERY (*if known*)　　　　PROOF　　　　TYPE

PRICE　　　　AGE STATEMENT (*if any*)　　　COLOR

## NOTES

*Check any that apply:*

- ☐ FLORAL
- ☐ WOODY
- ☐ LEATHER
- ☐ CITRUS
- ☐ GRASS

- ☐ SPICY
- ☐ SMOKY
- ☐ FRUITY
- ☐ SOLVENT/ASTRINGENT
- ☐ HONEY/CARAMEL

*Mark on the spectrum:*

SWEET　　　　　　　　　　　　DRY

← | | | | | | | | | | →
10　8　6　4　2　0　2　4　6　8　10

DELICATE　　　　　　　　　　BOLD

← | | | | | | | | | | →
10　8　6　4　2　0　2　4　6　8　10

SMOOTH　　　　　　　　　　INTENSE

← | | | | | | | | | | →
10　8　6　4　2　0　2　4　6　8　10

## OBSERVATIONS

## EVALUATION

| Y | N | |
|---|---|---|
| ☐ | ☐ | Recommend within category? |
| ☐ | ☐ | Recommend overall? |
| ☐ | ☐ | Interesting? |
| ☐ | ☐ | Unusual? |

THIS WHISKEY:

- ☐ Met expectations
- ☐ Exceeded expectations
- ☐ Disappointed

MY SCORE

1 to 10

IN A SINGLE WORD

# TASTING NOTES

| DATE | |
|------|--|
| LOCATION | |

**WHISKEY**

DISTILLERY (*if known*)        PROOF        TYPE

PRICE        AGE STATEMENT (*if any*)        COLOR

## NOTES

*Check any that apply:*

☐ FLORAL ☐ SPICY

☐ WOODY ☐ SMOKY

☐ LEATHER ☐ FRUITY

☐ CITRUS ☐ SOLVENT/ASTRINGENT

☐ GRASS ☐ HONEY/CARAMEL

*Mark on the spectrum:*

SWEET ←————————————→ DRY
10  8  6  4  2  0  2  4  6  8  10

DELICATE ←————————————→ BOLD
10  8  6  4  2  0  2  4  6  8  10

SMOOTH ←————————————→ INTENSE
10  8  6  4  2  0  2  4  6  8  10

## OBSERVATIONS

_____

_____

_____

_____

_____

_____

## EVALUATION

| Y | N | |
|---|---|--|
| ☐ | ☐ | Recommend within category? |
| ☐ | ☐ | Recommend overall? |
| ☐ | ☐ | Interesting? |
| ☐ | ☐ | Unusual? |

THIS WHISKEY:

☐ Met expectations

☐ Exceeded expectations

☐ Disappointed

MY SCORE

[    ]

1 to 10

IN A SINGLE WORD

# TASTING NOTES

| DATE | | WHISKEY | |
|------|--|---------|--|
| LOCATION | | | |

DISTILLERY (*if known*)　　　　PROOF　　　　TYPE

PRICE　　　　AGE STATEMENT (*if any*)　　　　COLOR

## NOTES

*Check any that apply:*

☐ FLORAL　　☐ SPICY

☐ WOODY　　☐ SMOKY

☐ LEATHER　☐ FRUITY

☐ CITRUS　　☐ SOLVENT/ASTRINGENT

☐ GRASS　　☐ HONEY/CARAMEL

*Mark on the spectrum:*

SWEET　　　　　　　　　　DRY
←　|　|　|　|　|　|　|　|　|　|　→
10　8　6　4　2　0　2　4　6　8　10

DELICATE　　　　　　　　BOLD
←　|　|　|　|　|　|　|　|　|　|　→
10　8　6　4　2　0　2　4　6　8　10

SMOOTH　　　　　　　　INTENSE
←　|　|　|　|　|　|　|　|　|　|　→
10　8　6　4　2　0　2　4　6　8　10

## OBSERVATIONS

_____

_____

_____

_____

_____

_____

## EVALUATION

| Y | N | | THIS WHISKEY: | MY SCORE |
|---|---|--|---------------|----------|
| ☐ | ☐ | Recommend within category? | ☐ Met expectations | |
| ☐ | ☐ | Recommend overall? | ☐ Exceeded expectations | |
| ☐ | ☐ | Interesting? | ☐ Disappointed | |
| ☐ | ☐ | Unusual? | | 1 to 10 |

IN A SINGLE WORD

# TASTING NOTES

| | |
|---|---|
| DATE | |
| LOCATION | |

**WHISKEY**

DISTILLERY (*if known*)      PROOF      TYPE

PRICE      AGE STATEMENT (*if any*)      COLOR

## NOTES

*Check any that apply:*

☐ FLORAL ☐ SPICY
☐ WOODY ☐ SMOKY
☐ LEATHER ☐ FRUITY
☐ CITRUS ☐ SOLVENT/ASTRINGENT
☐ GRASS ☐ HONEY/CARAMEL

*Mark on the spectrum:*

SWEET ← → DRY
10 8 6 4 2 0 2 4 6 8 10

DELICATE ← → BOLD
10 8 6 4 2 0 2 4 6 8 10

SMOOTH ← → INTENSE
10 8 6 4 2 0 2 4 6 8 10

## OBSERVATIONS

## EVALUATION

| Y | N | |
|---|---|---|
| ☐ | ☐ | Recommend within category? |
| ☐ | ☐ | Recommend overall? |
| ☐ | ☐ | Interesting? |
| ☐ | ☐ | Unusual? |

THIS WHISKEY:
☐ Met expectations
☐ Exceeded expectations
☐ Disappointed

MY SCORE

1 to 10

IN A SINGLE WORD

# TASTING NOTES

| DATE | |
|---|---|
| LOCATION | |

**WHISKEY**

DISTILLERY (*if known*)          PROOF          TYPE

PRICE          AGE STATEMENT (*if any*)          COLOR

## NOTES

*Check any that apply:*

☐ FLORAL   ☐ SPICY
☐ WOODY   ☐ SMOKY
☐ LEATHER   ☐ FRUITY
☐ CITRUS   ☐ SOLVENT/ASTRINGENT
☐ GRASS   ☐ HONEY/CARAMEL

*Mark on the spectrum:*

SWEET                                    DRY
←—|—|—|—|—|—|—|—|—|—|—→
10   8   6   4   2   0   2   4   6   8   10

DELICATE                              BOLD
←—|—|—|—|—|—|—|—|—|—|—→
10   8   6   4   2   0   2   4   6   8   10

SMOOTH                            INTENSE
←—|—|—|—|—|—|—|—|—|—|—→
10   8   6   4   2   0   2   4   6   8   10

## OBSERVATIONS

_____

_____

_____

_____

_____

_____

## EVALUATION

| Y | N | | THIS WHISKEY: | MY SCORE |
|---|---|---|---|---|
| ☐ | ☐ | Recommend within category? | ☐ Met expectations | |
| ☐ | ☐ | Recommend overall? | ☐ Exceeded expectations | |
| ☐ | ☐ | Interesting? | ☐ Disappointed | |
| ☐ | ☐ | Unusual? | | 1 to 10 |

IN A SINGLE WORD

# TASTING NOTES

| DATE | |
|---|---|
| LOCATION | |

**WHISKEY**

DISTILLERY (*if known*)          PROOF          TYPE

PRICE          AGE STATEMENT (*if any*)          COLOR

## NOTES

*Check any that apply:*

- ☐ FLORAL
- ☐ WOODY
- ☐ LEATHER
- ☐ CITRUS
- ☐ GRASS

- ☐ SPICY
- ☐ SMOKY
- ☐ FRUITY
- ☐ SOLVENT/ASTRINGENT
- ☐ HONEY/CARAMEL

*Mark on the spectrum:*

SWEET                                    DRY
10  8  6  4  2  0  2  4  6  8  10

DELICATE                                 BOLD
10  8  6  4  2  0  2  4  6  8  10

SMOOTH                               INTENSE
10  8  6  4  2  0  2  4  6  8  10

## OBSERVATIONS

## EVALUATION

| Y | N | | THIS WHISKEY: | MY SCORE |
|---|---|---|---|---|
| ☐ | ☐ | Recommend within category? | ☐ Met expectations | |
| ☐ | ☐ | Recommend overall? | ☐ Exceeded expectations | |
| ☐ | ☐ | Interesting? | ☐ Disappointed | |
| ☐ | ☐ | Unusual? | | 1 to 10 |

IN A SINGLE WORD

# TASTING NOTES

| | |
|---|---|
| DATE | |
| LOCATION | |

**WHISKEY**

DISTILLERY (*if known*)     PROOF     TYPE

PRICE     AGE STATEMENT (*if any*)     COLOR

## NOTES

*Check any that apply:*

☐ FLORAL    ☐ SPICY
☐ WOODY     ☐ SMOKY
☐ LEATHER   ☐ FRUITY
☐ CITRUS    ☐ SOLVENT/ASTRINGENT
☐ GRASS     ☐ HONEY/CARAMEL

*Mark on the spectrum:*

SWEET                                          DRY
←————+——+——+——+——+——+——+——+——+——→
10   8   6   4   2   0   2   4   6   8   10

DELICATE                                      BOLD
←————+——+——+——+——+——+——+——+——+——→
10   8   6   4   2   0   2   4   6   8   10

SMOOTH                                     INTENSE
←————+——+——+——+——+——+——+——+——+——→
10   8   6   4   2   0   2   4   6   8   10

## OBSERVATIONS

_____

_____

_____

_____

_____

_____

## EVALUATION

| Y | N | |
|---|---|---|
| ☐ | ☐ | Recommend within category? |
| ☐ | ☐ | Recommend overall? |
| ☐ | ☐ | Interesting? |
| ☐ | ☐ | Unusual? |

THIS WHISKEY:

☐ Met expectations
☐ Exceeded expectations
☐ Disappointed

**MY SCORE**

☐

1 to 10

IN A SINGLE WORD

# TASTING NOTES

| | |
|---|---|
| DATE | |
| LOCATION | |

**WHISKEY**

DISTILLERY (*if known*)　　　　PROOF　　　　TYPE

PRICE　　　　AGE STATEMENT (*if any*)　　　　COLOR

## NOTES

*Check any that apply:*

☐ FLORAL　　☐ SPICY
☐ WOODY　　☐ SMOKY
☐ LEATHER　☐ FRUITY
☐ CITRUS　　☐ SOLVENT/ASTRINGENT
☐ GRASS　　☐ HONEY/CARAMEL

*Mark on the spectrum:*

SWEET　　　　　　　　　　　　DRY
←—+—+—+—+—+—+—+—+—+—→
10　8　6　4　2　0　2　4　6　8　10

DELICATE　　　　　　　　　　BOLD
←—+—+—+—+—+—+—+—+—+—→
10　8　6　4　2　0　2　4　6　8　10

SMOOTH　　　　　　　　　INTENSE
←—+—+—+—+—+—+—+—+—+—→
10　8　6　4　2　0　2　4　6　8　10

## OBSERVATIONS

_____

_____

_____

_____

_____

_____

## EVALUATION

| Y | N | |
|---|---|---|
| ☐ | ☐ | Recommend within category? |
| ☐ | ☐ | Recommend overall? |
| ☐ | ☐ | Interesting? |
| ☐ | ☐ | Unusual? |

THIS WHISKEY:
☐ Met expectations
☐ Exceeded expectations
☐ Disappointed

MY SCORE

1 to 10

IN A SINGLE WORD

# TASTING NOTES

| DATE | |
|---|---|
| LOCATION | |

**WHISKEY**

DISTILLERY (*if known*)    PROOF    TYPE

PRICE    AGE STATEMENT (*if any*)    COLOR

## NOTES

*Check any that apply:*

☐ FLORAL  ☐ SPICY

☐ WOODY  ☐ SMOKY

☐ LEATHER  ☐ FRUITY

☐ CITRUS  ☐ SOLVENT/ASTRINGENT

☐ GRASS  ☐ HONEY/CARAMEL

*Mark on the spectrum:*

SWEET                                    DRY
← | | | | | | | | | →
10  8  6  4  2  0  2  4  6  8  10

DELICATE                                BOLD
← | | | | | | | | | →
10  8  6  4  2  0  2  4  6  8  10

SMOOTH                              INTENSE
← | | | | | | | | | →
10  8  6  4  2  0  2  4  6  8  10

## OBSERVATIONS

## EVALUATION

| Y | N | |
|---|---|---|
| ☐ | ☐ | Recommend within category? |
| ☐ | ☐ | Recommend overall? |
| ☐ | ☐ | Interesting? |
| ☐ | ☐ | Unusual? |

THIS WHISKEY:

☐ Met expectations

☐ Exceeded expectations

☐ Disappointed

MY SCORE

1 to 10

IN A SINGLE WORD

# TASTING NOTES

| | |
|---|---|
| DATE | |
| LOCATION | |

**WHISKEY**

DISTILLERY (*if known*)          PROOF          TYPE

PRICE          AGE STATEMENT (*if any*)          COLOR

## NOTES

*Check any that apply:*

☐ FLORAL      ☐ SPICY

☐ WOODY      ☐ SMOKY

☐ LEATHER    ☐ FRUITY

☐ CITRUS     ☐ SOLVENT/ASTRINGENT

☐ GRASS      ☐ HONEY/CARAMEL

*Mark on the spectrum:*

SWEET                                    DRY
10  8  6  4  2  0  2  4  6  8  10

DELICATE                                 BOLD
10  8  6  4  2  0  2  4  6  8  10

SMOOTH                               INTENSE
10  8  6  4  2  0  2  4  6  8  10

## OBSERVATIONS

_____

_____

_____

_____

_____

_____

## EVALUATION

| Y | N | | |
|---|---|---|---|
| ☐ | ☐ | Recommend within category? | |
| ☐ | ☐ | Recommend overall? | |
| ☐ | ☐ | Interesting? | |
| ☐ | ☐ | Unusual? | |

THIS WHISKEY:

☐ Met expectations
☐ Exceeded expectations
☐ Disappointed

MY SCORE

[    ]

1 to 10

IN A SINGLE WORD

# TASTING NOTES

| DATE | | |
|---|---|---|
| LOCATION | | |

**WHISKEY**

DISTILLERY (*if known*)          PROOF          TYPE

PRICE          AGE STATEMENT (*if any*)          COLOR

## NOTES

*Check any that apply:*

☐ FLORAL    ☐ SPICY
☐ WOODY    ☐ SMOKY
☐ LEATHER    ☐ FRUITY
☐ CITRUS    ☐ SOLVENT/ASTRINGENT
☐ GRASS    ☐ HONEY/CARAMEL

*Mark on the spectrum:*

SWEET                                   DRY
← + + + + + + + + + →
10  8  6  4  2  0  2  4  6  8  10

DELICATE                              BOLD
← + + + + + + + + + →
10  8  6  4  2  0  2  4  6  8  10

SMOOTH                            INTENSE
← + + + + + + + + + →
10  8  6  4  2  0  2  4  6  8  10

## OBSERVATIONS

_____
_____
_____
_____
_____
_____

## EVALUATION

| Y | N | |
|---|---|---|
| ☐ | ☐ | Recommend within category? |
| ☐ | ☐ | Recommend overall? |
| ☐ | ☐ | Interesting? |
| ☐ | ☐ | Unusual? |

THIS WHISKEY:
☐ Met expectations
☐ Exceeded expectations
☐ Disappointed

MY SCORE

[    ]

1 to 10

_____

IN A SINGLE WORD

# TASTING NOTES

DATE

LOCATION

**WHISKEY**

DISTILLERY *(if known)*  PROOF  TYPE

PRICE  AGE STATEMENT *(if any)*  COLOR

## NOTES

*Check any that apply:*

☐ FLORAL  ☐ SPICY

☐ WOODY  ☐ SMOKY

☐ LEATHER  ☐ FRUITY

☐ CITRUS  ☐ SOLVENT/ASTRINGENT

☐ GRASS  ☐ HONEY/CARAMEL

*Mark on the spectrum:*

SWEET  DRY

←|—|—|—|—|—|—|—|—|—|—|→
10  8  6  4  2  0  2  4  6  8  10

DELICATE  BOLD

←|—|—|—|—|—|—|—|—|—|—|→
10  8  6  4  2  0  2  4  6  8  10

SMOOTH  INTENSE

←|—|—|—|—|—|—|—|—|—|—|→
10  8  6  4  2  0  2  4  6  8  10

## OBSERVATIONS

## EVALUATION

| Y | N | | THIS WHISKEY: | MY SCORE |
|---|---|---|---|---|
| ☐ | ☐ | Recommend within category? | ☐ Met expectations | |
| ☐ | ☐ | Recommend overall? | ☐ Exceeded expectations | |
| ☐ | ☐ | Interesting? | ☐ Disappointed | |
| ☐ | ☐ | Unusual? | | 1 to 10 |

IN A SINGLE WORD

# TASTING NOTES

| DATE | | WHISKEY | |
|---|---|---|---|
| LOCATION | | | |

DISTILLERY *(if known)*          PROOF          TYPE

PRICE          AGE STATEMENT *(if any)*          COLOR

## NOTES

*Check any that apply:*

☐ FLORAL   ☐ SPICY
☐ WOODY   ☐ SMOKY
☐ LEATHER   ☐ FRUITY
☐ CITRUS   ☐ SOLVENT/ASTRINGENT
☐ GRASS   ☐ HONEY/CARAMEL

*Mark on the spectrum:*

SWEET                                              DRY
←—+—+—+—+—+—+—+—+—+—→
10   8    6    4    2    0    2    4    6    8   10

DELICATE                                          BOLD
←—+—+—+—+—+—+—+—+—+—→
10   8    6    4    2    0    2    4    6    8   10

SMOOTH                                        INTENSE
←—+—+—+—+—+—+—+—+—+—→
10   8    6    4    2    0    2    4    6    8   10

## OBSERVATIONS

_____

_____

_____

_____

_____

_____

## EVALUATION

| Y | N | | THIS WHISKEY: | MY SCORE |
|---|---|---|---|---|
| ☐ | ☐ | Recommend within category? | ☐ Met expectations | |
| ☐ | ☐ | Recommend overall? | ☐ Exceeded expectations | |
| ☐ | ☐ | Interesting? | ☐ Disappointed | |
| ☐ | ☐ | Unusual? | | 1 to 10 |

IN A SINGLE WORD _____

# TASTING NOTES

| DATE | | WHISKEY | |
|------|--|---------|--|
| LOCATION | | | |

DISTILLERY (*if known*)　　　　　PROOF　　　　TYPE

PRICE　　　　AGE STATEMENT (*if any*)　　COLOR

## NOTES

*Check any that apply:*

☐ FLORAL　　☐ SPICY

☐ WOODY　　☐ SMOKY

☐ LEATHER　☐ FRUITY

☐ CITRUS　　☐ SOLVENT/ASTRINGENT

☐ GRASS　　☐ HONEY/CARAMEL

*Mark on the spectrum:*

SWEET　　　　　　　　　　　　　　DRY
←——+——+——+——+——+——+——+——+——+——→
10　8　6　4　2　0　2　4　6　8　10

DELICATE　　　　　　　　　　　　BOLD
←——+——+——+——+——+——+——+——+——+——→
10　8　6　4　2　0　2　4　6　8　10

SMOOTH　　　　　　　　　　　INTENSE
←——+——+——+——+——+——+——+——+——+——→
10　8　6　4　2　0　2　4　6　8　10

## OBSERVATIONS

_____

_____

_____

_____

_____

_____

## EVALUATION

| Y | N | | THIS WHISKEY: | MY SCORE |
|---|---|--|---------------|----------|
| ☐ | ☐ | Recommend within category? | ☐ Met expectations | |
| ☐ | ☐ | Recommend overall? | ☐ Exceeded expectations | |
| ☐ | ☐ | Interesting? | ☐ Disappointed | |
| ☐ | ☐ | Unusual? | | 1 to 10 |

IN A SINGLE WORD _____

# TASTING NOTES

| DATE | |
|---|---|
| LOCATION | |

**WHISKEY** [                    ]

DISTILLERY (*if known*)      PROOF      TYPE

PRICE      AGE STATEMENT (*if any*)      COLOR

## NOTES

*Check any that apply:*

- ☐ FLORAL
- ☐ WOODY
- ☐ LEATHER
- ☐ CITRUS
- ☐ GRASS

- ☐ SPICY
- ☐ SMOKY
- ☐ FRUITY
- ☐ SOLVENT/ASTRINGENT
- ☐ HONEY/CARAMEL

*Mark on the spectrum:*

SWEET      DRY

←——+——+——+——+——+——+——+——+——+——→
10   8   6   4   2   0   2   4   6   8   10

DELICATE      BOLD

←——+——+——+——+——+——+——+——+——+——→
10   8   6   4   2   0   2   4   6   8   10

SMOOTH      INTENSE

←——+——+——+——+——+——+——+——+——+——→
10   8   6   4   2   0   2   4   6   8   10

## OBSERVATIONS

_____

_____

_____

_____

_____

_____

## EVALUATION

| Y | N | |
|---|---|---|
| ☐ | ☐ | Recommend within category? |
| ☐ | ☐ | Recommend overall? |
| ☐ | ☐ | Interesting? |
| ☐ | ☐ | Unusual? |

THIS WHISKEY:
- ☐ Met expectations
- ☐ Exceeded expectations
- ☐ Disappointed

MY SCORE

[      ]

1 to 10

IN A SINGLE WORD

# TASTING NOTES

| DATE | | WHISKEY | |
|------|--|---------|--|
| LOCATION | | | |

DISTILLERY (*if known*)         PROOF         TYPE

PRICE         AGE STATEMENT (*if any*)         COLOR

## NOTES

*Check any that apply:*

☐ FLORAL    ☐ SPICY
☐ WOODY     ☐ SMOKY
☐ LEATHER   ☐ FRUITY
☐ CITRUS    ☐ SOLVENT/ASTRINGENT
☐ GRASS     ☐ HONEY/CARAMEL

*Mark on the spectrum:*

SWEET                                    DRY
←—+—+—+—+—+—+—+—+—+—+—→
10  8   6   4   2   0   2   4   6   8  10

DELICATE                                 BOLD
←—+—+—+—+—+—+—+—+—+—+—→
10  8   6   4   2   0   2   4   6   8  10

SMOOTH                                INTENSE
←—+—+—+—+—+—+—+—+—+—+—→
10  8   6   4   2   0   2   4   6   8  10

## OBSERVATIONS

_____

_____

_____

_____

_____

_____

## EVALUATION

| Y | N | | THIS WHISKEY: | MY SCORE |
|---|---|--|---------------|----------|
| ☐ | ☐ | Recommend within category? | ☐ Met expectations | |
| ☐ | ☐ | Recommend overall? | ☐ Exceeded expectations | |
| ☐ | ☐ | Interesting? | ☐ Disappointed | |
| ☐ | ☐ | Unusual? | | 1 to 10 |

IN A SINGLE WORD

# TASTING NOTES

| DATE | |
|---|---|
| LOCATION | |

**WHISKEY**

DISTILLERY (*if known*)            PROOF            TYPE

PRICE            AGE STATEMENT (*if any*)            COLOR

## NOTES

*Check any that apply:*

☐ FLORAL          ☐ SPICY
☐ WOODY           ☐ SMOKY
☐ LEATHER         ☐ FRUITY
☐ CITRUS          ☐ SOLVENT/ASTRINGENT
☐ GRASS           ☐ HONEY/CARAMEL

*Mark on the spectrum:*

SWEET                                    DRY
← + + + + + + + + + + →
10  8   6   4   2   0   2   4   6   8   10

DELICATE                                 BOLD
← + + + + + + + + + + →
10  8   6   4   2   0   2   4   6   8   10

SMOOTH                                INTENSE
← + + + + + + + + + + →
10  8   6   4   2   0   2   4   6   8   10

## OBSERVATIONS

_____

_____

_____

_____

_____

_____

## EVALUATION

| Y | N | |
|---|---|---|
| ☐ | ☐ | Recommend within category? |
| ☐ | ☐ | Recommend overall? |
| ☐ | ☐ | Interesting? |
| ☐ | ☐ | Unusual? |

THIS WHISKEY:
☐ Met expectations
☐ Exceeded expectations
☐ Disappointed

MY SCORE

☐

1 to 10

_____

IN A SINGLE WORD

# TASTING NOTES

| DATE | |
|------|--|
| LOCATION | |

**WHISKEY**

DISTILLERY (*if known*)  PROOF  TYPE

PRICE  AGE STATEMENT (*if any*)  COLOR

## NOTES

*Check any that apply:*

☐ FLORAL ☐ SPICY

☐ WOODY ☐ SMOKY

☐ LEATHER ☐ FRUITY

☐ CITRUS ☐ SOLVENT/ASTRINGENT

☐ GRASS ☐ HONEY/CARAMEL

*Mark on the spectrum:*

SWEET                                      DRY
10  8  6  4  2  0  2  4  6  8  10

DELICATE                                  BOLD
10  8  6  4  2  0  2  4  6  8  10

SMOOTH                                INTENSE
10  8  6  4  2  0  2  4  6  8  10

## OBSERVATIONS

## EVALUATION

| Y | N | |
|---|---|--|
| ☐ | ☐ | Recommend within category? |
| ☐ | ☐ | Recommend overall? |
| ☐ | ☐ | Interesting? |
| ☐ | ☐ | Unusual? |

THIS WHISKEY:

☐ Met expectations

☐ Exceeded expectations

☐ Disappointed

MY SCORE

1 to 10

IN A SINGLE WORD

# TASTING NOTES

| DATE | |
|---|---|
| LOCATION | |

**WHISKEY**

DISTILLERY (if known)　　　　PROOF　　　TYPE

PRICE　　　AGE STATEMENT (if any)　　　COLOR

## NOTES

Check any that apply:

☐ FLORAL　☐ SPICY
☐ WOODY　☐ SMOKY
☐ LEATHER　☐ FRUITY
☐ CITRUS　☐ SOLVENT/ASTRINGENT
☐ GRASS　☐ HONEY/CARAMEL

Mark on the spectrum:

SWEET　　　　　　　　　　　　DRY
← + + + + + + + + + + →
10　8　6　4　2　0　2　4　6　8　10

DELICATE　　　　　　　　　　BOLD
← + + + + + + + + + + →
10　8　6　4　2　0　2　4　6　8　10

SMOOTH　　　　　　　　　INTENSE
← + + + + + + + + + + →
10　8　6　4　2　0　2　4　6　8　10

## OBSERVATIONS

## EVALUATION

| Y | N | | THIS WHISKEY: | MY SCORE |
|---|---|---|---|---|
| ☐ | ☐ | Recommend within category? | ☐ Met expectations | |
| ☐ | ☐ | Recommend overall? | ☐ Exceeded expectations | |
| ☐ | ☐ | Interesting? | ☐ Disappointed | |
| ☐ | ☐ | Unusual? | | 1 to 10 |

IN A SINGLE WORD

# TASTING NOTES

| DATE | |
|------|---|
| LOCATION | |

**WHISKEY**

DISTILLERY (*if known*)          PROOF          TYPE

PRICE          AGE STATEMENT (*if any*)          COLOR

## NOTES

*Check any that apply:*

☐ FLORAL      ☐ SPICY

☐ WOODY      ☐ SMOKY

☐ LEATHER    ☐ FRUITY

☐ CITRUS     ☐ SOLVENT/ASTRINGENT

☐ GRASS      ☐ HONEY/CARAMEL

*Mark on the spectrum:*

SWEET                                    DRY

←——+——+——+——+——+——+——+——+——+——→
10   8   6   4   2   0   2   4   6   8   10

DELICATE                                 BOLD

←——+——+——+——+——+——+——+——+——+——→
10   8   6   4   2   0   2   4   6   8   10

SMOOTH                                INTENSE

←——+——+——+——+——+——+——+——+——+——→
10   8   6   4   2   0   2   4   6   8   10

## OBSERVATIONS

_____

_____

_____

_____

_____

_____

_____

## EVALUATION

| Y | N | |
|---|---|---|
| ☐ | ☐ | Recommend within category? |
| ☐ | ☐ | Recommend overall? |
| ☐ | ☐ | Interesting? |
| ☐ | ☐ | Unusual? |

THIS WHISKEY:

☐ Met expectations

☐ Exceeded expectations

☐ Disappointed

MY SCORE

[     ]

1 to 10

IN A SINGLE WORD

# TASTING NOTES

| DATE | | WHISKEY | |
|------|---|---------|---|
| LOCATION | | | |

DISTILLERY (*if known*)      PROOF      TYPE

PRICE      AGE STATEMENT (*if any*)      COLOR

## NOTES

*Check any that apply:*

☐ FLORAL    ☐ SPICY
☐ WOODY    ☐ SMOKY
☐ LEATHER    ☐ FRUITY
☐ CITRUS    ☐ SOLVENT/ASTRINGENT
☐ GRASS    ☐ HONEY/CARAMEL

*Mark on the spectrum:*

SWEET        DRY
← | | | | | | | | | | →
10   8   6   4   2   0   2   4   6   8   10

DELICATE        BOLD
← | | | | | | | | | | →
10   8   6   4   2   0   2   4   6   8   10

SMOOTH        INTENSE
← | | | | | | | | | | →
10   8   6   4   2   0   2   4   6   8   10

## OBSERVATIONS

_____

_____

_____

_____

_____

_____

## EVALUATION

| Y | N | |
|---|---|---|
| ☐ | ☐ | Recommend within category? |
| ☐ | ☐ | Recommend overall? |
| ☐ | ☐ | Interesting? |
| ☐ | ☐ | Unusual? |

THIS WHISKEY:
☐ Met expectations
☐ Exceeded expectations
☐ Disappointed

MY SCORE

[ ]

1 to 10

IN A SINGLE WORD

# TASTING NOTES

| DATE | | WHISKEY | |
|------|--|---------|--|
| LOCATION | | | |

DISTILLERY (*if known*)        PROOF        TYPE

PRICE        AGE STATEMENT (*if any*)        COLOR

## NOTES

*Check any that apply:*

☐ FLORAL      ☐ SPICY
☐ WOODY       ☐ SMOKY
☐ LEATHER     ☐ FRUITY
☐ CITRUS      ☐ SOLVENT/ASTRINGENT
☐ GRASS       ☐ HONEY/CARAMEL

*Mark on the spectrum:*

SWEET                                      DRY
←—+—+—+—+—+—+—+—+—+—→
10  8   6   4   2   0   2   4   6   8   10

DELICATE                                   BOLD
←—+—+—+—+—+—+—+—+—+—→
10  8   6   4   2   0   2   4   6   8   10

SMOOTH                                 INTENSE
←—+—+—+—+—+—+—+—+—+—→
10  8   6   4   2   0   2   4   6   8   10

## OBSERVATIONS

_____

_____

_____

_____

_____

_____

## EVALUATION

| Y | N | | |
|---|---|--|--|
| ☐ | ☐ | Recommend within category? | |
| ☐ | ☐ | Recommend overall? | |
| ☐ | ☐ | Interesting? | |
| ☐ | ☐ | Unusual? | |

THIS WHISKEY:
☐ Met expectations
☐ Exceeded expectations
☐ Disappointed

MY SCORE

☐

1 to 10

IN A SINGLE WORD

# TASTING NOTES

| DATE | |
|------|--|
| LOCATION | |

**WHISKEY**

DISTILLERY (*if known*)  PROOF  TYPE

PRICE  AGE STATEMENT (*if any*)  COLOR

## NOTES

*Check any that apply:*

☐ FLORAL  ☐ SPICY
☐ WOODY  ☐ SMOKY
☐ LEATHER  ☐ FRUITY
☐ CITRUS  ☐ SOLVENT/ASTRINGENT
☐ GRASS  ☐ HONEY/CARAMEL

*Mark on the spectrum:*

SWEET ← 10 8 6 4 2 0 2 4 6 8 10 → DRY

DELICATE ← 10 8 6 4 2 0 2 4 6 8 10 → BOLD

SMOOTH ← 10 8 6 4 2 0 2 4 6 8 10 → INTENSE

## OBSERVATIONS

_____

_____

_____

_____

_____

_____

## EVALUATION

| Y | N | |
|---|---|--|
| ☐ | ☐ | Recommend within category? |
| ☐ | ☐ | Recommend overall? |
| ☐ | ☐ | Interesting? |
| ☐ | ☐ | Unusual? |

THIS WHISKEY:
☐ Met expectations
☐ Exceeded expectations
☐ Disappointed

MY SCORE

1 to 10

IN A SINGLE WORD

# TASTING NOTES

| DATE | |
|---|---|
| LOCATION | |

**WHISKEY**

DISTILLERY (*if known*)          PROOF          TYPE

PRICE          AGE STATEMENT (*if any*)          COLOR

## NOTES

*Check any that apply:*

- ☐ FLORAL
- ☐ WOODY
- ☐ LEATHER
- ☐ CITRUS
- ☐ GRASS

- ☐ SPICY
- ☐ SMOKY
- ☐ FRUITY
- ☐ SOLVENT/ASTRINGENT
- ☐ HONEY/CARAMEL

*Mark on the spectrum:*

SWEET                                    DRY
←—+—+—+—+—+—+—+—+—+—→
10  8  6  4  2  0  2  4  6  8  10

DELICATE                              BOLD
←—+—+—+—+—+—+—+—+—+—→
10  8  6  4  2  0  2  4  6  8  10

SMOOTH                            INTENSE
←—+—+—+—+—+—+—+—+—+—→
10  8  6  4  2  0  2  4  6  8  10

## OBSERVATIONS

_____

_____

_____

_____

_____

_____

## EVALUATION

| Y | N | | THIS WHISKEY: | MY SCORE |
|---|---|---|---|---|
| ☐ | ☐ | Recommend within category? | ☐ Met expectations | |
| ☐ | ☐ | Recommend overall? | ☐ Exceeded expectations | |
| ☐ | ☐ | Interesting? | ☐ Disappointed | |
| ☐ | ☐ | Unusual? | | 1 to 10 |

IN A SINGLE WORD

# TASTING NOTES

| DATE | |
|---|---|
| LOCATION | |

**WHISKEY**

DISTILLERY (*if known*)  PROOF  TYPE

PRICE  AGE STATEMENT (*if any*)  COLOR

## NOTES

*Check any that apply:*

☐ FLORAL  ☐ SPICY
☐ WOODY  ☐ SMOKY
☐ LEATHER  ☐ FRUITY
☐ CITRUS  ☐ SOLVENT/ASTRINGENT
☐ GRASS  ☐ HONEY/CARAMEL

*Mark on the spectrum:*

SWEET                    DRY
←—+—+—+—+—+—+—+—+—+—→
10  8  6  4  2  0  2  4  6  8  10

DELICATE                 BOLD
←—+—+—+—+—+—+—+—+—+—→
10  8  6  4  2  0  2  4  6  8  10

SMOOTH                 INTENSE
←—+—+—+—+—+—+—+—+—+—→
10  8  6  4  2  0  2  4  6  8  10

## OBSERVATIONS

_____
_____
_____
_____
_____
_____

## EVALUATION

| Y | N | |
|---|---|---|
| ☐ | ☐ | Recommend within category? |
| ☐ | ☐ | Recommend overall? |
| ☐ | ☐ | Interesting? |
| ☐ | ☐ | Unusual? |

THIS WHISKEY:
☐ Met expectations
☐ Exceeded expectations
☐ Disappointed

MY SCORE

[ ]

1 to 10

IN A SINGLE WORD

# TASTING NOTES

| DATE | | |
|---|---|---|
| LOCATION | | |

**WHISKEY**

DISTILLERY (*if known*)          PROOF          TYPE

PRICE          AGE STATEMENT (*if any*)          COLOR

## NOTES

*Check any that apply:*

☐ FLORAL    ☐ SPICY

☐ WOODY    ☐ SMOKY

☐ LEATHER    ☐ FRUITY

☐ CITRUS    ☐ SOLVENT/ASTRINGENT

☐ GRASS    ☐ HONEY/CARAMEL

*Mark on the spectrum:*

SWEET          DRY

← 10 8 6 4 2 0 2 4 6 8 10 →

DELICATE          BOLD

← 10 8 6 4 2 0 2 4 6 8 10 →

SMOOTH          INTENSE

← 10 8 6 4 2 0 2 4 6 8 10 →

## OBSERVATIONS

## EVALUATION

| Y | N | |
|---|---|---|
| ☐ | ☐ | Recommend within category? |
| ☐ | ☐ | Recommend overall? |
| ☐ | ☐ | Interesting? |
| ☐ | ☐ | Unusual? |

THIS WHISKEY:

☐ Met expectations

☐ Exceeded expectations

☐ Disappointed

MY SCORE

1 to 10

IN A SINGLE WORD

# TASTING NOTES

| DATE |
|------|
| LOCATION |

**WHISKEY**

DISTILLERY (*if known*)                    PROOF          TYPE

PRICE              AGE STATEMENT (*if any*)          COLOR

## NOTES

*Check any that apply:*

☐ FLORAL       ☐ SPICY
☐ WOODY        ☐ SMOKY
☐ LEATHER      ☐ FRUITY
☐ CITRUS       ☐ SOLVENT/ASTRINGENT
☐ GRASS        ☐ HONEY/CARAMEL

*Mark on the spectrum:*

SWEET                                   DRY
← | | | | | | | | | | →
10  8  6  4  2  0  2  4  6  8  10

DELICATE                                BOLD
← | | | | | | | | | | →
10  8  6  4  2  0  2  4  6  8  10

SMOOTH                              INTENSE
← | | | | | | | | | | →
10  8  6  4  2  0  2  4  6  8  10

## OBSERVATIONS

_____

_____

_____

_____

_____

_____

## EVALUATION

| Y | N | |
|---|---|---|
| ☐ | ☐ | Recommend within category? |
| ☐ | ☐ | Recommend overall? |
| ☐ | ☐ | Interesting? |
| ☐ | ☐ | Unusual? |

THIS WHISKEY:

☐ Met expectations
☐ Exceeded expectations
☐ Disappointed

MY SCORE

1 to 10

IN A SINGLE WORD

# TASTING NOTES

| DATE | |
|------|--|
| LOCATION | |

**WHISKEY**

DISTILLERY (*if known*)        PROOF        TYPE

PRICE        AGE STATEMENT (*if any*)        COLOR

## NOTES

*Check any that apply:*

- ☐ FLORAL
- ☐ WOODY
- ☐ LEATHER
- ☐ CITRUS
- ☐ GRASS

- ☐ SPICY
- ☐ SMOKY
- ☐ FRUITY
- ☐ SOLVENT/ASTRINGENT
- ☐ HONEY/CARAMEL

*Mark on the spectrum:*

SWEET                                   DRY

←——+——+——+——+——+——+——+——+——+——→
10   8   6   4   2   0   2   4   6   8   10

DELICATE                              BOLD

←——+——+——+——+——+——+——+——+——+——→
10   8   6   4   2   0   2   4   6   8   10

SMOOTH                            INTENSE

←——+——+——+——+——+——+——+——+——+——→
10   8   6   4   2   0   2   4   6   8   10

## OBSERVATIONS

_____

_____

_____

_____

_____

_____

## EVALUATION

| Y | N | |
|---|---|--|
| ☐ | ☐ | Recommend within category? |
| ☐ | ☐ | Recommend overall? |
| ☐ | ☐ | Interesting? |
| ☐ | ☐ | Unusual? |

THIS WHISKEY:
- ☐ Met expectations
- ☐ Exceeded expectations
- ☐ Disappointed

MY SCORE

[    ]

1 to 10

_____
IN A SINGLE WORD

# TASTING NOTES

| DATE | | | |
|------|--|--|--|
| LOCATION | | **WHISKEY** | |

DISTILLERY (*if known*)         PROOF         TYPE

PRICE         AGE STATEMENT (*if any*)         COLOR

## NOTES

*Check any that apply:*

☐ FLORAL    ☐ SPICY

☐ WOODY    ☐ SMOKY

☐ LEATHER    ☐ FRUITY

☐ CITRUS    ☐ SOLVENT/ASTRINGENT

☐ GRASS    ☐ HONEY/CARAMEL

*Mark on the spectrum:*

SWEET                                              DRY

10  8  6  4  2  0  2  4  6  8  10

DELICATE                                          BOLD

10  8  6  4  2  0  2  4  6  8  10

SMOOTH                                          INTENSE

10  8  6  4  2  0  2  4  6  8  10

## OBSERVATIONS

## EVALUATION

| Y | N | | THIS WHISKEY: | MY SCORE |
|---|---|--|---------------|----------|
| ☐ | ☐ | Recommend within category? | ☐ Met expectations | |
| ☐ | ☐ | Recommend overall? | ☐ Exceeded expectations | |
| ☐ | ☐ | Interesting? | ☐ Disappointed | |
| ☐ | ☐ | Unusual? | | 1 to 10 |

IN A SINGLE WORD

# TASTING NOTES

| DATE | |
|------|--|
| LOCATION | |

**WHISKEY** [ ]

DISTILLERY (*if known*)     PROOF     TYPE

PRICE     AGE STATEMENT (*if any*)     COLOR

## NOTES

*Check any that apply:*

☐ FLORAL     ☐ SPICY
☐ WOODY      ☐ SMOKY
☐ LEATHER    ☐ FRUITY
☐ CITRUS     ☐ SOLVENT/ASTRINGENT
☐ GRASS      ☐ HONEY/CARAMEL

*Mark on the spectrum:*

SWEET                                    DRY
←——+——+——+——+——+——+——+——+——+——→
10   8   6   4   2   0   2   4   6   8   10

DELICATE                                 BOLD
←——+——+——+——+——+——+——+——+——+——→
10   8   6   4   2   0   2   4   6   8   10

SMOOTH                                INTENSE
←——+——+——+——+——+——+——+——+——+——→
10   8   6   4   2   0   2   4   6   8   10

## OBSERVATIONS

_____
_____
_____
_____
_____
_____

## EVALUATION

| Y | N | | |
|---|---|---|---|
| ☐ | ☐ | Recommend within category? | |
| ☐ | ☐ | Recommend overall? | |
| ☐ | ☐ | Interesting? | |
| ☐ | ☐ | Unusual? | |

THIS WHISKEY:
☐ Met expectations
☐ Exceeded expectations
☐ Disappointed

MY SCORE
[ ]
1 to 10

IN A SINGLE WORD

# TASTING NOTES

| DATE | |
|------|-|
| LOCATION | |

**WHISKEY**

DISTILLERY (*if known*)          PROOF          TYPE

PRICE          AGE STATEMENT (*if any*)          COLOR

## NOTES

*Check any that apply:*

☐ FLORAL      ☐ SPICY
☐ WOODY       ☐ SMOKY
☐ LEATHER     ☐ FRUITY
☐ CITRUS      ☐ SOLVENT/ASTRINGENT
☐ GRASS       ☐ HONEY/CARAMEL

*Mark on the spectrum:*

SWEET                                    DRY
10  8  6  4  2  0  2  4  6  8  10

DELICATE                                 BOLD
10  8  6  4  2  0  2  4  6  8  10

SMOOTH                                INTENSE
10  8  6  4  2  0  2  4  6  8  10

## OBSERVATIONS

## EVALUATION

| Y | N | |
|---|---|-|
| ☐ | ☐ | Recommend within category? |
| ☐ | ☐ | Recommend overall? |
| ☐ | ☐ | Interesting? |
| ☐ | ☐ | Unusual? |

THIS WHISKEY:
☐ Met expectations
☐ Exceeded expectations
☐ Disappointed

MY SCORE

1 to 10

IN A SINGLE WORD

# TASTING NOTES

| DATE | |
|---|---|
| LOCATION | |

**WHISKEY**

DISTILLERY (*if known*)          PROOF          TYPE

PRICE          AGE STATEMENT (*if any*)          COLOR

## NOTES

*Check any that apply:*

☐ FLORAL    ☐ SPICY
☐ WOODY     ☐ SMOKY
☐ LEATHER   ☐ FRUITY
☐ CITRUS    ☐ SOLVENT/ASTRINGENT
☐ GRASS     ☐ HONEY/CARAMEL

*Mark on the spectrum:*

SWEET                                    DRY
← + + + + + + + + + + →
10  8  6  4  2  0  2  4  6  8  10

DELICATE                                 BOLD
← + + + + + + + + + + →
10  8  6  4  2  0  2  4  6  8  10

SMOOTH                                INTENSE
← + + + + + + + + + + →
10  8  6  4  2  0  2  4  6  8  10

## OBSERVATIONS

_____

_____

_____

_____

_____

_____

## EVALUATION

| Y | N | |
|---|---|---|
| ☐ | ☐ | Recommend within category? |
| ☐ | ☐ | Recommend overall? |
| ☐ | ☐ | Interesting? |
| ☐ | ☐ | Unusual? |

THIS WHISKEY:
☐ Met expectations
☐ Exceeded expectations
☐ Disappointed

MY SCORE

[ ]

1 to 10

_____

IN A SINGLE WORD

# TASTING NOTES

| DATE | |
|---|---|
| LOCATION | |

**WHISKEY**

DISTILLERY (*if known*)  PROOF  TYPE

PRICE  AGE STATEMENT (*if any*)  COLOR

## NOTES

*Check any that apply:*

☐ FLORAL  ☐ SPICY
☐ WOODY  ☐ SMOKY
☐ LEATHER  ☐ FRUITY
☐ CITRUS  ☐ SOLVENT/ASTRINGENT
☐ GRASS  ☐ HONEY/CARAMEL

*Mark on the spectrum:*

SWEET                                  DRY
←——+——+——+——+——+——+——+——+——+——→
10   8   6   4   2   0   2   4   6   8   10

DELICATE                              BOLD
←——+——+——+——+——+——+——+——+——+——→
10   8   6   4   2   0   2   4   6   8   10

SMOOTH                            INTENSE
←——+——+——+——+——+——+——+——+——+——→
10   8   6   4   2   0   2   4   6   8   10

## OBSERVATIONS

## EVALUATION

| Y | N | | THIS WHISKEY: | MY SCORE |
|---|---|---|---|---|
| ☐ | ☐ | Recommend within category? | ☐ Met expectations | |
| ☐ | ☐ | Recommend overall? | ☐ Exceeded expectations | |
| ☐ | ☐ | Interesting? | ☐ Disappointed | |
| ☐ | ☐ | Unusual? | | 1 to 10 |

IN A SINGLE WORD

# TASTING NOTES

| DATE | |
|---|---|
| LOCATION | |

**WHISKEY** [                    ]

DISTILLERY (*if known*)          PROOF          TYPE

PRICE          AGE STATEMENT (*if any*)          COLOR

## NOTES

*Check any that apply:*

☐ FLORAL    ☐ SPICY
☐ WOODY     ☐ SMOKY
☐ LEATHER   ☐ FRUITY
☐ CITRUS    ☐ SOLVENT/ASTRINGENT
☐ GRASS     ☐ HONEY/CARAMEL

*Mark on the spectrum:*

SWEET                                    DRY
←—+—+—+—+—+—+—+—+—+—+—→
10  8  6  4  2  0  2  4  6  8  10

DELICATE                                 BOLD
←—+—+—+—+—+—+—+—+—+—+—→
10  8  6  4  2  0  2  4  6  8  10

SMOOTH                               INTENSE
←—+—+—+—+—+—+—+—+—+—+—→
10  8  6  4  2  0  2  4  6  8  10

## OBSERVATIONS

_____
_____
_____
_____
_____
_____

## EVALUATION

| Y | N | | THIS WHISKEY: | MY SCORE |
|---|---|---|---|---|
| ☐ | ☐ | Recommend within category? | ☐ Met expectations | |
| ☐ | ☐ | Recommend overall? | ☐ Exceeded expectations | |
| ☐ | ☐ | Interesting? | ☐ Disappointed | |
| ☐ | ☐ | Unusual? | | 1 to 10 |

IN A SINGLE WORD

# TASTING NOTES

| DATE | |
|---|---|
| LOCATION | |

**WHISKEY**

DISTILLERY (*if known*)          PROOF          TYPE

PRICE          AGE STATEMENT (*if any*)          COLOR

## NOTES

*Check any that apply:*

☐ FLORAL   ☐ SPICY
☐ WOODY   ☐ SMOKY
☐ LEATHER   ☐ FRUITY
☐ CITRUS   ☐ SOLVENT/ASTRINGENT
☐ GRASS   ☐ HONEY/CARAMEL

*Mark on the spectrum:*

SWEET                                              DRY
←——+——+——+——+——+——+——+——+——+——→
10   8   6   4   2   0   2   4   6   8   10

DELICATE                                        BOLD
←——+——+——+——+——+——+——+——+——+——→
10   8   6   4   2   0   2   4   6   8   10

SMOOTH                                       INTENSE
←——+——+——+——+——+——+——+——+——+——→
10   8   6   4   2   0   2   4   6   8   10

## OBSERVATIONS

_____

_____

_____

_____

_____

_____

## EVALUATION

| Y | N | | THIS WHISKEY: | MY SCORE |
|---|---|---|---|---|
| ☐ | ☐ | Recommend within category? | ☐ Met expectations | |
| ☐ | ☐ | Recommend overall? | ☐ Exceeded expectations | |
| ☐ | ☐ | Interesting? | ☐ Disappointed | |
| ☐ | ☐ | Unusual? | | 1 to 10 |

_____

IN A SINGLE WORD

# TASTING NOTES

| DATE | |
|------|--|
| LOCATION | |

**WHISKEY**

DISTILLERY (*if known*)　　　　　PROOF　　　TYPE

PRICE　　　AGE STATEMENT (*if any*)　　COLOR

## NOTES

Check any that apply:

☐ FLORAL ☐ SPICY
☐ WOODY ☐ SMOKY
☐ LEATHER ☐ FRUITY
☐ CITRUS ☐ SOLVENT/ASTRINGENT
☐ GRASS ☐ HONEY/CARAMEL

Mark on the spectrum:

SWEET　　　　　　　　　　DRY
←—+—+—+—+—+—+—+—+—+—→
10　8　6　4　2　0　2　4　6　8　10

DELICATE　　　　　　　　BOLD
←—+—+—+—+—+—+—+—+—+—→
10　8　6　4　2　0　2　4　6　8　10

SMOOTH　　　　　　　INTENSE
←—+—+—+—+—+—+—+—+—+—→
10　8　6　4　2　0　2　4　6　8　10

## OBSERVATIONS

_____
_____
_____
_____
_____
_____

## EVALUATION

| Y | N | | |
|---|---|---|---|
| ☐ | ☐ | Recommend within category? | |
| ☐ | ☐ | Recommend overall? | |
| ☐ | ☐ | Interesting? | |
| ☐ | ☐ | Unusual? | |

THIS WHISKEY:
☐ Met expectations
☐ Exceeded expectations
☐ Disappointed

MY SCORE

[ ]

1 to 10

_____
IN A SINGLE WORD

# TASTING NOTES

| DATE | |
|---|---|
| LOCATION | |

**WHISKEY**

DISTILLERY (*if known*)          PROOF          TYPE

PRICE          AGE STATEMENT (*if any*)          COLOR

## NOTES

*Check any that apply:*

☐ FLORAL    ☐ SPICY

☐ WOODY     ☐ SMOKY

☐ LEATHER   ☐ FRUITY

☐ CITRUS    ☐ SOLVENT/ASTRINGENT

☐ GRASS     ☐ HONEY/CARAMEL

*Mark on the spectrum:*

SWEET                                          DRY
←———+———+———+———+———+———+———+———+———+———→
10   8   6   4   2   0   2   4   6   8   10

DELICATE                                       BOLD
←———+———+———+———+———+———+———+———+———+———→
10   8   6   4   2   0   2   4   6   8   10

SMOOTH                                      INTENSE
←———+———+———+———+———+———+———+———+———+———→
10   8   6   4   2   0   2   4   6   8   10

## OBSERVATIONS

_____

_____

_____

_____

_____

_____

## EVALUATION

| Y | N | |
|---|---|---|
| ☐ | ☐ | Recommend within category? |
| ☐ | ☐ | Recommend overall? |
| ☐ | ☐ | Interesting? |
| ☐ | ☐ | Unusual? |

THIS WHISKEY:

☐ Met expectations

☐ Exceeded expectations

☐ Disappointed

MY SCORE

[        ]

1 to 10

_____

IN A SINGLE WORD

# TASTING NOTES

| DATE | |
|---|---|
| LOCATION | |

**WHISKEY**

DISTILLERY (*if known*)  PROOF  TYPE

PRICE  AGE STATEMENT (*if any*)  COLOR

## NOTES

*Check any that apply:*

☐ FLORAL  ☐ SPICY
☐ WOODY  ☐ SMOKY
☐ LEATHER  ☐ FRUITY
☐ CITRUS  ☐ SOLVENT/ASTRINGENT
☐ GRASS  ☐ HONEY/CARAMEL

*Mark on the spectrum:*

SWEET ← → DRY
10  8  6  4  2  0  2  4  6  8  10

DELICATE ← → BOLD
10  8  6  4  2  0  2  4  6  8  10

SMOOTH ← → INTENSE
10  8  6  4  2  0  2  4  6  8  10

## OBSERVATIONS

## EVALUATION

| Y | N | |
|---|---|---|
| ☐ | ☐ | Recommend within category? |
| ☐ | ☐ | Recommend overall? |
| ☐ | ☐ | Interesting? |
| ☐ | ☐ | Unusual? |

THIS WHISKEY:
☐ Met expectations
☐ Exceeded expectations
☐ Disappointed

MY SCORE

1 to 10

IN A SINGLE WORD

# TASTING NOTES

| DATE | |
|------|--|
| LOCATION | |

**WHISKEY**

DISTILLERY (*if known*)  PROOF  TYPE

PRICE  AGE STATEMENT (*if any*)  COLOR

## NOTES

*Check any that apply:*

☐ FLORAL ☐ SPICY
☐ WOODY ☐ SMOKY
☐ LEATHER ☐ FRUITY
☐ CITRUS ☐ SOLVENT/ASTRINGENT
☐ GRASS ☐ HONEY/CARAMEL

*Mark on the spectrum:*

SWEET ←——————————————→ DRY
10  8  6  4  2  0  2  4  6  8  10

DELICATE ←——————————————→ BOLD
10  8  6  4  2  0  2  4  6  8  10

SMOOTH ←——————————————→ INTENSE
10  8  6  4  2  0  2  4  6  8  10

## OBSERVATIONS

_____

_____

_____

_____

_____

_____

## EVALUATION

| Y | N | |
|---|---|--|
| ☐ | ☐ | Recommend within category? |
| ☐ | ☐ | Recommend overall? |
| ☐ | ☐ | Interesting? |
| ☐ | ☐ | Unusual? |

THIS WHISKEY:
☐ Met expectations
☐ Exceeded expectations
☐ Disappointed

MY SCORE

1 to 10

IN A SINGLE WORD

# TASTING NOTES

| DATE | | | |
|------|---|---|---|
| LOCATION | | **WHISKEY** | |

DISTILLERY *(if known)*       PROOF       TYPE

PRICE       AGE STATEMENT *(if any)*       COLOR

## NOTES

*Check any that apply:*

- ☐ FLORAL
- ☐ WOODY
- ☐ LEATHER
- ☐ CITRUS
- ☐ GRASS

- ☐ SPICY
- ☐ SMOKY
- ☐ FRUITY
- ☐ SOLVENT/ASTRINGENT
- ☐ HONEY/CARAMEL

*Mark on the spectrum:*

SWEET                    DRY
←   +   +   +   +   +   +   +   +   +   +   →
10   8   6   4   2   0   2   4   6   8   10

DELICATE                BOLD
←   +   +   +   +   +   +   +   +   +   +   →
10   8   6   4   2   0   2   4   6   8   10

SMOOTH              INTENSE
←   +   +   +   +   +   +   +   +   +   +   →
10   8   6   4   2   0   2   4   6   8   10

## OBSERVATIONS

## EVALUATION

| Y | N | | |
|---|---|---|---|
| ☐ | ☐ | Recommend within category? | |
| ☐ | ☐ | Recommend overall? | |
| ☐ | ☐ | Interesting? | |
| ☐ | ☐ | Unusual? | |

THIS WHISKEY:
- ☐ Met expectations
- ☐ Exceeded expectations
- ☐ Disappointed

MY SCORE

1 to 10

IN A SINGLE WORD

# TASTING NOTES

| DATE | |
|---|---|
| LOCATION | |

**WHISKEY**

DISTILLERY (*if known*)      PROOF      TYPE

PRICE      AGE STATEMENT (*if any*)      COLOR

## NOTES

*Check any that apply:*

☐ FLORAL    ☐ SPICY

☐ WOODY    ☐ SMOKY

☐ LEATHER    ☐ FRUITY

☐ CITRUS    ☐ SOLVENT/ASTRINGENT

☐ GRASS    ☐ HONEY/CARAMEL

*Mark on the spectrum:*

SWEET                    DRY

←—+—+—+—+—+—+—+—+—+—→

10   8   6   4   2   0   2   4   6   8   10

DELICATE             BOLD

←—+—+—+—+—+—+—+—+—+—→

10   8   6   4   2   0   2   4   6   8   10

SMOOTH            INTENSE

←—+—+—+—+—+—+—+—+—+—→

10   8   6   4   2   0   2   4   6   8   10

## OBSERVATIONS

## EVALUATION

| Y | N | | |
|---|---|---|---|
| ☐ | ☐ | Recommend within category? | |
| ☐ | ☐ | Recommend overall? | |
| ☐ | ☐ | Interesting? | |
| ☐ | ☐ | Unusual? | |

THIS WHISKEY:

☐ Met expectations

☐ Exceeded expectations

☐ Disappointed

MY SCORE

1 to 10

IN A SINGLE WORD

# TASTING NOTES

| DATE | |
|---|---|
| LOCATION | **WHISKEY** |

DISTILLERY *(if known)*          PROOF          TYPE

PRICE          AGE STATEMENT *(if any)*          COLOR

## NOTES

*Check any that apply:*

- ☐ FLORAL
- ☐ WOODY
- ☐ LEATHER
- ☐ CITRUS
- ☐ GRASS

- ☐ SPICY
- ☐ SMOKY
- ☐ FRUITY
- ☐ SOLVENT/ASTRINGENT
- ☐ HONEY/CARAMEL

*Mark on the spectrum:*

SWEET                                        DRY
← | | | | | | | | | | →
10   8   6   4   2   0   2   4   6   8   10

DELICATE                                    BOLD
← | | | | | | | | | | →
10   8   6   4   2   0   2   4   6   8   10

SMOOTH                                  INTENSE
← | | | | | | | | | | →
10   8   6   4   2   0   2   4   6   8   10

## OBSERVATIONS

_____
_____
_____
_____
_____
_____

## EVALUATION

| Y | N | | |
|---|---|---|---|
| ☐ | ☐ | Recommend within category? | |
| ☐ | ☐ | Recommend overall? | |
| ☐ | ☐ | Interesting? | |
| ☐ | ☐ | Unusual? | |

THIS WHISKEY:
- ☐ Met expectations
- ☐ Exceeded expectations
- ☐ Disappointed

MY SCORE

[   ]

1 to 10

IN A SINGLE WORD

# TASTING NOTES

| DATE | |
|---|---|
| LOCATION | |

**WHISKEY**

DISTILLERY (*if known*)　　　　PROOF　　　　TYPE

PRICE　　　　AGE STATEMENT (*if any*)　　　　COLOR

## NOTES

*Check any that apply:*

☐ FLORAL　☐ SPICY

☐ WOODY　☐ SMOKY

☐ LEATHER　☐ FRUITY

☐ CITRUS　☐ SOLVENT/ASTRINGENT

☐ GRASS　☐ HONEY/CARAMEL

*Mark on the spectrum:*

SWEET　　　　　　　　　　　　DRY

←――+――+――+――+――+――+――+――+――→
10　8　6　4　2　0　2　4　6　8　10

DELICATE　　　　　　　　　　BOLD

←――+――+――+――+――+――+――+――+――→
10　8　6　4　2　0　2　4　6　8　10

SMOOTH　　　　　　　　　　INTENSE

←――+――+――+――+――+――+――+――+――→
10　8　6　4　2　0　2　4　6　8　10

## OBSERVATIONS

_____

_____

_____

_____

_____

_____

## EVALUATION

| Y | N | | THIS WHISKEY: | MY SCORE |
|---|---|---|---|---|
| ☐ | ☐ | Recommend within category? | ☐ Met expectations | |
| ☐ | ☐ | Recommend overall? | ☐ Exceeded expectations | |
| ☐ | ☐ | Interesting? | ☐ Disappointed | |
| ☐ | ☐ | Unusual? | | 1 to 10 |

IN A SINGLE WORD

# TASTING NOTES

| DATE | | | WHISKEY | |
|---|---|---|---|---|
| LOCATION | | | | |

DISTILLERY (*if known*)      PROOF      TYPE

PRICE      AGE STATEMENT (*if any*)      COLOR

## NOTES

*Check any that apply:*

☐ FLORAL      ☐ SPICY

☐ WOODY      ☐ SMOKY

☐ LEATHER      ☐ FRUITY

☐ CITRUS      ☐ SOLVENT/ASTRINGENT

☐ GRASS      ☐ HONEY/CARAMEL

*Mark on the spectrum:*

SWEET                      DRY

←—+—+—+—+—+—+—+—+—+—+—→

10   8   6   4   2   0   2   4   6   8   10

DELICATE                  BOLD

←—+—+—+—+—+—+—+—+—+—+—→

10   8   6   4   2   0   2   4   6   8   10

SMOOTH                 INTENSE

←—+—+—+—+—+—+—+—+—+—+—→

10   8   6   4   2   0   2   4   6   8   10

## OBSERVATIONS

_____

_____

_____

_____

_____

_____

## EVALUATION

| Y | N | | THIS WHISKEY: | MY SCORE |
|---|---|---|---|---|
| ☐ | ☐ | Recommend within category? | ☐ Met expectations | |
| ☐ | ☐ | Recommend overall? | ☐ Exceeded expectations | |
| ☐ | ☐ | Interesting? | ☐ Disappointed | |
| ☐ | ☐ | Unusual? | | 1 to 10 |

IN A SINGLE WORD

# TASTING NOTES

| DATE | | WHISKEY | |
|------|--|---------|--|
| LOCATION | | | |

DISTILLERY (if known)          PROOF          TYPE

PRICE          AGE STATEMENT (if any)          COLOR

## NOTES

*Check any that apply:*

☐ FLORAL    ☐ SPICY

☐ WOODY    ☐ SMOKY

☐ LEATHER    ☐ FRUITY

☐ CITRUS    ☐ SOLVENT/ASTRINGENT

☐ GRASS    ☐ HONEY/CARAMEL

*Mark on the spectrum:*

SWEET                 DRY

← 10  8  6  4  2  0  2  4  6  8  10 →

DELICATE             BOLD

← 10  8  6  4  2  0  2  4  6  8  10 →

SMOOTH            INTENSE

← 10  8  6  4  2  0  2  4  6  8  10 →

## OBSERVATIONS

_____

_____

_____

_____

_____

_____

## EVALUATION

Y   N

☐   ☐   Recommend within category?

☐   ☐   Recommend overall?

☐   ☐   Interesting?

☐   ☐   Unusual?

THIS WHISKEY:

☐ Met expectations

☐ Exceeded expectations

☐ Disappointed

MY SCORE

1 to 10

IN A SINGLE WORD

# TASTING NOTES

| DATE | |
|---|---|
| LOCATION | |

**WHISKEY**

DISTILLERY (*if known*)   PROOF   TYPE

PRICE   AGE STATEMENT (*if any*)   COLOR

## NOTES

*Check any that apply:*

☐ FLORAL   ☐ SPICY
☐ WOODY   ☐ SMOKY
☐ LEATHER   ☐ FRUITY
☐ CITRUS   ☐ SOLVENT/ASTRINGENT
☐ GRASS   ☐ HONEY/CARAMEL

*Mark on the spectrum:*

SWEET   DRY
←——+——+——+——+——+——+——+——+——+——→
10   8   6   4   2   0   2   4   6   8   10

DELICATE   BOLD
←——+——+——+——+——+——+——+——+——+——→
10   8   6   4   2   0   2   4   6   8   10

SMOOTH   INTENSE
←——+——+——+——+——+——+——+——+——+——→
10   8   6   4   2   0   2   4   6   8   10

## OBSERVATIONS

## EVALUATION

| Y | N | |
|---|---|---|
| ☐ | ☐ | Recommend within category? |
| ☐ | ☐ | Recommend overall? |
| ☐ | ☐ | Interesting? |
| ☐ | ☐ | Unusual? |

THIS WHISKEY:
☐ Met expectations
☐ Exceeded expectations
☐ Disappointed

MY SCORE

1 to 10

IN A SINGLE WORD

# TASTING NOTES

| DATE | |
|---|---|
| LOCATION | |

**WHISKEY**

_____    _____    _____

DISTILLERY (*if known*)      PROOF      TYPE

_____    _____    _____

PRICE      AGE STATEMENT (*if any*)      COLOR

## NOTES

*Check any that apply:*

☐ FLORAL    ☐ SPICY
☐ WOODY    ☐ SMOKY
☐ LEATHER    ☐ FRUITY
☐ CITRUS    ☐ SOLVENT/ASTRINGENT
☐ GRASS    ☐ HONEY/CARAMEL

*Mark on the spectrum:*

SWEET      DRY
← + + + + + + + + + + →
10   8   6   4   2   0   2   4   6   8   10

DELICATE      BOLD
← + + + + + + + + + + →
10   8   6   4   2   0   2   4   6   8   10

SMOOTH      INTENSE
← + + + + + + + + + + →
10   8   6   4   2   0   2   4   6   8   10

## OBSERVATIONS

_____

_____

_____

_____

_____

_____

## EVALUATION

| Y | N | |
|---|---|---|
| ☐ | ☐ | Recommend within category? |
| ☐ | ☐ | Recommend overall? |
| ☐ | ☐ | Interesting? |
| ☐ | ☐ | Unusual? |

THIS WHISKEY:
☐ Met expectations
☐ Exceeded expectations
☐ Disappointed

MY SCORE

[ ]

1 to 10

_____

IN A SINGLE WORD

# TASTING NOTES

| DATE | | |
|------|---|---|
| LOCATION | **WHISKEY** | |

---

DISTILLERY (*if known*)   PROOF   TYPE

---

PRICE   AGE STATEMENT (*if any*)   COLOR

## NOTES

*Check any that apply:*

☐ FLORAL ☐ SPICY

☐ WOODY ☐ SMOKY

☐ LEATHER ☐ FRUITY

☐ CITRUS ☐ SOLVENT/ASTRINGENT

☐ GRASS ☐ HONEY/CARAMEL

*Mark on the spectrum:*

SWEET                                          DRY
←—+—+—+—+—+—+—+—+—+—+—→
10   8   6   4   2   0   2   4   6   8   10

DELICATE                                      BOLD
←—+—+—+—+—+—+—+—+—+—+—→
10   8   6   4   2   0   2   4   6   8   10

SMOOTH                                     INTENSE
←—+—+—+—+—+—+—+—+—+—+—→
10   8   6   4   2   0   2   4   6   8   10

## OBSERVATIONS

---

---

---

---

---

---

## EVALUATION

| Y | N | | THIS WHISKEY: | MY SCORE |
|---|---|---|---|---|
| ☐ | ☐ | Recommend within category? | ☐ Met expectations | |
| ☐ | ☐ | Recommend overall? | ☐ Exceeded expectations | |
| ☐ | ☐ | Interesting? | ☐ Disappointed | |
| ☐ | ☐ | Unusual? | | 1 to 10 |

---

IN A SINGLE WORD

# TASTING NOTES

| DATE | |
|---|---|
| LOCATION | |

**WHISKEY**

DISTILLERY (*if known*)  PROOF  TYPE

PRICE  AGE STATEMENT (*if any*)  COLOR

## NOTES

*Check any that apply:*

☐ FLORAL  ☐ SPICY
☐ WOODY  ☐ SMOKY
☐ LEATHER  ☐ FRUITY
☐ CITRUS  ☐ SOLVENT/ASTRINGENT
☐ GRASS  ☐ HONEY/CARAMEL

*Mark on the spectrum:*

SWEET  DRY
10  8  6  4  2  0  2  4  6  8  10

DELICATE  BOLD
10  8  6  4  2  0  2  4  6  8  10

SMOOTH  INTENSE
10  8  6  4  2  0  2  4  6  8  10

## OBSERVATIONS

_____

_____

_____

_____

_____

_____

## EVALUATION

| Y | N | |
|---|---|---|
| ☐ | ☐ | Recommend within category? |
| ☐ | ☐ | Recommend overall? |
| ☐ | ☐ | Interesting? |
| ☐ | ☐ | Unusual? |

THIS WHISKEY:
☐ Met expectations
☐ Exceeded expectations
☐ Disappointed

MY SCORE

1 to 10

IN A SINGLE WORD

# TASTING NOTES

| DATE | |
|---|---|
| LOCATION | |

**WHISKEY**

DISTILLERY (*if known*)  PROOF  TYPE

PRICE  AGE STATEMENT (*if any*)  COLOR

## NOTES

*Check any that apply:*

☐ FLORAL  ☐ SPICY

☐ WOODY  ☐ SMOKY

☐ LEATHER  ☐ FRUITY

☐ CITRUS  ☐ SOLVENT/ASTRINGENT

☐ GRASS  ☐ HONEY/CARAMEL

*Mark on the spectrum:*

SWEET  DRY

←—+—+—+—+—+—+—+—+—+—→
10  8  6  4  2  0  2  4  6  8  10

DELICATE  BOLD

←—+—+—+—+—+—+—+—+—+—→
10  8  6  4  2  0  2  4  6  8  10

SMOOTH  INTENSE

←—+—+—+—+—+—+—+—+—+—→
10  8  6  4  2  0  2  4  6  8  10

## OBSERVATIONS

## EVALUATION

| Y | N | | THIS WHISKEY: | MY SCORE |
|---|---|---|---|---|
| ☐ | ☐ | Recommend within category? | ☐ Met expectations | |
| ☐ | ☐ | Recommend overall? | ☐ Exceeded expectations | |
| ☐ | ☐ | Interesting? | ☐ Disappointed | |
| ☐ | ☐ | Unusual? | | 1 to 10 |

IN A SINGLE WORD

# TASTING NOTES

| DATE | |
|---|---|
| LOCATION | |

WHISKEY

DISTILLERY (*if known*)      PROOF      TYPE

PRICE      AGE STATEMENT (*if any*)      COLOR

## NOTES

*Check any that apply:*

☐ FLORAL    ☐ SPICY
☐ WOODY    ☐ SMOKY
☐ LEATHER    ☐ FRUITY
☐ CITRUS    ☐ SOLVENT/ASTRINGENT
☐ GRASS    ☐ HONEY/CARAMEL

*Mark on the spectrum:*

SWEET            DRY
← | | | | | | | | | | →
10   8   6   4   2   0   2   4   6   8   10

DELICATE          BOLD
← | | | | | | | | | | →
10   8   6   4   2   0   2   4   6   8   10

SMOOTH         INTENSE
← | | | | | | | | | | →
10   8   6   4   2   0   2   4   6   8   10

## OBSERVATIONS

_____

_____

_____

_____

_____

_____

## EVALUATION

| Y | N | |
|---|---|---|
| ☐ | ☐ | Recommend within category? |
| ☐ | ☐ | Recommend overall? |
| ☐ | ☐ | Interesting? |
| ☐ | ☐ | Unusual? |

THIS WHISKEY:
☐ Met expectations
☐ Exceeded expectations
☐ Disappointed

MY SCORE

1 to 10

IN A SINGLE WORD

# TASTING NOTES

| DATE | | WHISKEY |
| --- | --- | --- |
| LOCATION | | |

DISTILLERY *(if known)*    PROOF    TYPE

PRICE    AGE STATEMENT *(if any)*    COLOR

## NOTES

*Check any that apply:*

☐ FLORAL ☐ SPICY
☐ WOODY ☐ SMOKY
☐ LEATHER ☐ FRUITY
☐ CITRUS ☐ SOLVENT/ASTRINGENT
☐ GRASS ☐ HONEY/CARAMEL

*Mark on the spectrum:*

SWEET                                      DRY
←—+—+—+—+—+—+—+—+—+—→
10  8  6  4  2  0  2  4  6  8  10

DELICATE                                   BOLD
←—+—+—+—+—+—+—+—+—+—→
10  8  6  4  2  0  2  4  6  8  10

SMOOTH                                  INTENSE
←—+—+—+—+—+—+—+—+—+—→
10  8  6  4  2  0  2  4  6  8  10

## OBSERVATIONS

## EVALUATION

| Y | N | | THIS WHISKEY: | MY SCORE |
| --- | --- | --- | --- | --- |
| ☐ | ☐ | Recommend within category? | ☐ Met expectations | |
| ☐ | ☐ | Recommend overall? | ☐ Exceeded expectations | |
| ☐ | ☐ | Interesting? | ☐ Disappointed | |
| ☐ | ☐ | Unusual? | | 1 to 10 |

IN A SINGLE WORD

# TASTING NOTES

| DATE | |
|---|---|
| LOCATION | |

**WHISKEY**

DISTILLERY (*if known*)　　　　PROOF　　　TYPE

PRICE　　　AGE STATEMENT (*if any*)　　COLOR

## NOTES

*Check any that apply:*

☐ FLORAL　☐ SPICY

☐ WOODY　☐ SMOKY

☐ LEATHER　☐ FRUITY

☐ CITRUS　☐ SOLVENT/ASTRINGENT

☐ GRASS　☐ HONEY/CARAMEL

*Mark on the spectrum:*

SWEET　　　　　　　　　　　DRY

← + + + + + + + + + →
10　8　6　4　2　0　2　4　6　8　10

DELICATE　　　　　　　　　BOLD

← + + + + + + + + + →
10　8　6　4　2　0　2　4　6　8　10

SMOOTH　　　　　　　　INTENSE

← + + + + + + + + + →
10　8　6　4　2　0　2　4　6　8　10

## OBSERVATIONS

## EVALUATION

| Y | N | | THIS WHISKEY: | MY SCORE |
|---|---|---|---|---|
| ☐ | ☐ | Recommend within category? | ☐ Met expectations | |
| ☐ | ☐ | Recommend overall? | ☐ Exceeded expectations | |
| ☐ | ☐ | Interesting? | ☐ Disappointed | |
| ☐ | ☐ | Unusual? | | 1 to 10 |

IN A SINGLE WORD

# TASTING NOTES

| DATE | |
|---|---|
| LOCATION | |

**WHISKEY** [                    ]

DISTILLERY (*if known*)      PROOF      TYPE

PRICE      AGE STATEMENT (*if any*)      COLOR

## NOTES

*Check any that apply:*

☐ FLORAL    ☐ SPICY
☐ WOODY    ☐ SMOKY
☐ LEATHER    ☐ FRUITY
☐ CITRUS    ☐ SOLVENT/ASTRINGENT
☐ GRASS    ☐ HONEY/CARAMEL

*Mark on the spectrum:*

SWEET ←————————————→ DRY
10  8  6  4  2  0  2  4  6  8  10

DELICATE ←————————————→ BOLD
10  8  6  4  2  0  2  4  6  8  10

SMOOTH ←————————————→ INTENSE
10  8  6  4  2  0  2  4  6  8  10

## OBSERVATIONS

_____

_____

_____

_____

_____

_____

## EVALUATION

| Y | N | | |
|---|---|---|---|
| ☐ | ☐ | Recommend within category? | |
| ☐ | ☐ | Recommend overall? | |
| ☐ | ☐ | Interesting? | |
| ☐ | ☐ | Unusual? | |

THIS WHISKEY:
☐ Met expectations
☐ Exceeded expectations
☐ Disappointed

MY SCORE
[        ]
1 to 10

IN A SINGLE WORD

# TASTING NOTES

| DATE | |
|---|---|
| LOCATION | |

**WHISKEY**

---

DISTILLERY (*if known*)          PROOF          TYPE

---

PRICE          AGE STATEMENT (*if any*)          COLOR

## NOTES

*Check any that apply:*

☐ FLORAL    ☐ SPICY

☐ WOODY    ☐ SMOKY

☐ LEATHER    ☐ FRUITY

☐ CITRUS    ☐ SOLVENT/ASTRINGENT

☐ GRASS    ☐ HONEY/CARAMEL

*Mark on the spectrum:*

SWEET                                          DRY
←—+—+—+—+—+—+—+—+—+—→
10  8   6   4   2   0   2   4   6   8   10

DELICATE                                       BOLD
←—+—+—+—+—+—+—+—+—+—→
10  8   6   4   2   0   2   4   6   8   10

SMOOTH                                      INTENSE
←—+—+—+—+—+—+—+—+—+—→
10  8   6   4   2   0   2   4   6   8   10

## OBSERVATIONS

---
---
---
---
---
---

## EVALUATION

| Y | N | |
|---|---|---|
| ☐ | ☐ | Recommend within category? |
| ☐ | ☐ | Recommend overall? |
| ☐ | ☐ | Interesting? |
| ☐ | ☐ | Unusual? |

THIS WHISKEY:

☐ Met expectations

☐ Exceeded expectations

☐ Disappointed

**MY SCORE**

1 to 10

IN A SINGLE WORD

# TASTING NOTES

| DATE | | WHISKEY | |
|------|--|---------|--|
| LOCATION | | | |

DISTILLERY *(if known)*        PROOF        TYPE

PRICE        AGE STATEMENT *(if any)*        COLOR

## NOTES

*Check any that apply:*

☐ FLORAL      ☐ SPICY

☐ WOODY       ☐ SMOKY

☐ LEATHER     ☐ FRUITY

☐ CITRUS      ☐ SOLVENT/ASTRINGENT

☐ GRASS       ☐ HONEY/CARAMEL

*Mark on the spectrum:*

SWEET                                  DRY
← 10  8  6  4  2  0  2  4  6  8  10 →

DELICATE                               BOLD
← 10  8  6  4  2  0  2  4  6  8  10 →

SMOOTH                              INTENSE
← 10  8  6  4  2  0  2  4  6  8  10 →

## OBSERVATIONS

## EVALUATION

| Y | N | | THIS WHISKEY: | MY SCORE |
|---|---|--|---------------|----------|
| ☐ | ☐ | Recommend within category? | ☐ Met expectations | |
| ☐ | ☐ | Recommend overall? | ☐ Exceeded expectations | |
| ☐ | ☐ | Interesting? | ☐ Disappointed | |
| ☐ | ☐ | Unusual? | | 1 to 10 |

IN A SINGLE WORD

# TASTING NOTES

| DATE | |
|------|--|
| LOCATION | |

**WHISKEY**

DISTILLERY (*if known*)　　　　PROOF　　　　TYPE

PRICE　　　　AGE STATEMENT (*if any*)　　　COLOR

## NOTES

*Check any that apply:*

☐ FLORAL　　☐ SPICY
☐ WOODY　　☐ SMOKY
☐ LEATHER　☐ FRUITY
☐ CITRUS　　☐ SOLVENT/ASTRINGENT
☐ GRASS　　☐ HONEY/CARAMEL

*Mark on the spectrum:*

SWEET　　　　　　　　　　　　　DRY
←—+—+—+—+—+—+—+—+—+—→
10　8　6　4　2　0　2　4　6　8　10

DELICATE　　　　　　　　　　　BOLD
←—+—+—+—+—+—+—+—+—+—→
10　8　6　4　2　0　2　4　6　8　10

SMOOTH　　　　　　　　　　　INTENSE
←—+—+—+—+—+—+—+—+—+—→
10　8　6　4　2　0　2　4　6　8　10

## OBSERVATIONS

_____

_____

_____

_____

_____

_____

## EVALUATION

| Y | N | | THIS WHISKEY: | MY SCORE |
|---|---|--|---------------|----------|
| ☐ | ☐ | Recommend within category? | ☐ Met expectations | |
| ☐ | ☐ | Recommend overall? | ☐ Exceeded expectations | |
| ☐ | ☐ | Interesting? | ☐ Disappointed | |
| ☐ | ☐ | Unusual? | | 1 to 10 |

IN A SINGLE WORD

# TASTING NOTES

| DATE | WHISKEY |
|------|---------|
| LOCATION | |

DISTILLERY (*if known*)          PROOF          TYPE

PRICE          AGE STATEMENT (*if any*)          COLOR

## NOTES

*Check any that apply:*

☐ FLORAL    ☐ SPICY

☐ WOODY     ☐ SMOKY

☐ LEATHER   ☐ FRUITY

☐ CITRUS    ☐ SOLVENT/ASTRINGENT

☐ GRASS     ☐ HONEY/CARAMEL

*Mark on the spectrum:*

SWEET                                    DRY
←  |  |  |  |  |  |  |  |  |  →
10  8  6  4  2  0  2  4  6  8  10

DELICATE                                BOLD
←  |  |  |  |  |  |  |  |  |  →
10  8  6  4  2  0  2  4  6  8  10

SMOOTH                              INTENSE
←  |  |  |  |  |  |  |  |  |  →
10  8  6  4  2  0  2  4  6  8  10

## OBSERVATIONS

_____

_____

_____

_____

_____

_____

## EVALUATION

| Y | N | | THIS WHISKEY: | MY SCORE |
|---|---|---|---|---|
| ☐ | ☐ | Recommend within category? | ☐ Met expectations | |
| ☐ | ☐ | Recommend overall? | ☐ Exceeded expectations | |
| ☐ | ☐ | Interesting? | ☐ Disappointed | |
| ☐ | ☐ | Unusual? | | 1 to 10 |

IN A SINGLE WORD

# TASTING NOTES

| DATE |
|------|
| LOCATION |

**WHISKEY**

_____
DISTILLERY (*if known*)          PROOF          TYPE

_____
PRICE          AGE STATEMENT (*if any*)          COLOR

## NOTES

*Check any that apply:*

☐ FLORAL          ☐ SPICY
☐ WOODY           ☐ SMOKY
☐ LEATHER         ☐ FRUITY
☐ CITRUS          ☐ SOLVENT/ASTRINGENT
☐ GRASS           ☐ HONEY/CARAMEL

*Mark on the spectrum:*

SWEET                                              DRY
←—+—+—+—+—+—+—+—+—+—→
10   8   6   4   2   0   2   4   6   8   10

DELICATE                                          BOLD
←—+—+—+—+—+—+—+—+—+—→
10   8   6   4   2   0   2   4   6   8   10

SMOOTH                                         INTENSE
←—+—+—+—+—+—+—+—+—+—→
10   8   6   4   2   0   2   4   6   8   10

## OBSERVATIONS

_____
_____
_____
_____
_____
_____

## EVALUATION

| Y | N | |
|---|---|---|
| ☐ | ☐ | Recommend within category? |
| ☐ | ☐ | Recommend overall? |
| ☐ | ☐ | Interesting? |
| ☐ | ☐ | Unusual? |

THIS WHISKEY:
☐ Met expectations
☐ Exceeded expectations
☐ Disappointed

MY SCORE

☐

1 to 10

_____
IN A SINGLE WORD

# TASTING NOTES

| DATE | |
|---|---|
| LOCATION | |

**WHISKEY**

DISTILLERY (*if known*)      PROOF      TYPE

PRICE      AGE STATEMENT (*if any*)      COLOR

## NOTES

*Check any that apply:*

☐ FLORAL    ☐ SPICY

☐ WOODY    ☐ SMOKY

☐ LEATHER    ☐ FRUITY

☐ CITRUS    ☐ SOLVENT/ASTRINGENT

☐ GRASS    ☐ HONEY/CARAMEL

*Mark on the spectrum:*

SWEET                DRY

← +—+—+—+—+—+—+—+—+—+ →
10   8   6   4   2   0   2   4   6   8   10

DELICATE            BOLD

← +—+—+—+—+—+—+—+—+—+ →
10   8   6   4   2   0   2   4   6   8   10

SMOOTH           INTENSE

← +—+—+—+—+—+—+—+—+—+ →
10   8   6   4   2   0   2   4   6   8   10

## OBSERVATIONS

_____

_____

_____

_____

_____

_____

## EVALUATION

| Y | N | | THIS WHISKEY: | MY SCORE |
|---|---|---|---|---|
| ☐ | ☐ | Recommend within category? | ☐ Met expectations | |
| ☐ | ☐ | Recommend overall? | ☐ Exceeded expectations | |
| ☐ | ☐ | Interesting? | ☐ Disappointed | |
| ☐ | ☐ | Unusual? | | 1 to 10 |

IN A SINGLE WORD

# TASTING NOTES

| DATE |
|------|
| LOCATION |

**WHISKEY**

DISTILLERY (if known)      PROOF      TYPE

PRICE      AGE STATEMENT (if any)      COLOR

## NOTES

*Check any that apply:*

☐ FLORAL      ☐ SPICY
☐ WOODY       ☐ SMOKY
☐ LEATHER     ☐ FRUITY
☐ CITRUS      ☐ SOLVENT/ASTRINGENT
☐ GRASS       ☐ HONEY/CARAMEL

*Mark on the spectrum:*

SWEET                                    DRY
←—+—+—+—+—+—+—+—+—+—→
10  8   6   4   2   0   2   4   6   8   10

DELICATE                                BOLD
←—+—+—+—+—+—+—+—+—+—→
10  8   6   4   2   0   2   4   6   8   10

SMOOTH                               INTENSE
←—+—+—+—+—+—+—+—+—+—→
10  8   6   4   2   0   2   4   6   8   10

## OBSERVATIONS

_____

_____

_____

_____

_____

_____

## EVALUATION

| Y | N | |
|---|---|---|
| ☐ | ☐ | Recommend within category? |
| ☐ | ☐ | Recommend overall? |
| ☐ | ☐ | Interesting? |
| ☐ | ☐ | Unusual? |

THIS WHISKEY:
☐ Met expectations
☐ Exceeded expectations
☐ Disappointed

MY SCORE

[ ]

1 to 10

IN A SINGLE WORD

# TASTING NOTES

| DATE | |
|------|---|
| LOCATION | |

**WHISKEY**

DISTILLERY (*if known*)          PROOF          TYPE

PRICE          AGE STATEMENT (*if any*)          COLOR

## NOTES

*Check any that apply:*

☐ FLORAL    ☐ SPICY

☐ WOODY    ☐ SMOKY

☐ LEATHER    ☐ FRUITY

☐ CITRUS    ☐ SOLVENT/ASTRINGENT

☐ GRASS    ☐ HONEY/CARAMEL

*Mark on the spectrum:*

SWEET                                    DRY
← | | | | | | | | | →
10  8  6  4  2  0  2  4  6  8  10

DELICATE                                BOLD
← | | | | | | | | | →
10  8  6  4  2  0  2  4  6  8  10

SMOOTH                              INTENSE
← | | | | | | | | | →
10  8  6  4  2  0  2  4  6  8  10

## OBSERVATIONS

_____

_____

_____

_____

_____

_____

## EVALUATION

| Y | N | | |
|---|---|---|---|
| ☐ | ☐ | Recommend within category? | |
| ☐ | ☐ | Recommend overall? | |
| ☐ | ☐ | Interesting? | |
| ☐ | ☐ | Unusual? | |

THIS WHISKEY:

☐ Met expectations

☐ Exceeded expectations

☐ Disappointed

MY SCORE

[     ]

1 to 10

_____

IN A SINGLE WORD

# TASTING NOTES

| DATE | |
|------|--|
| LOCATION | |

**WHISKEY**

DISTILLERY (*if known*)      PROOF      TYPE

PRICE      AGE STATEMENT (*if any*)      COLOR

## NOTES

*Check any that apply:*

☐ FLORAL      ☐ SPICY
☐ WOODY       ☐ SMOKY
☐ LEATHER     ☐ FRUITY
☐ CITRUS      ☐ SOLVENT/ASTRINGENT
☐ GRASS       ☐ HONEY/CARAMEL

*Mark on the spectrum:*

SWEET                          DRY
10  8  6  4  2  0  2  4  6  8  10

DELICATE                       BOLD
10  8  6  4  2  0  2  4  6  8  10

SMOOTH                      INTENSE
10  8  6  4  2  0  2  4  6  8  10

## OBSERVATIONS

_____

_____

_____

_____

_____

_____

## EVALUATION

| Y | N | |
|---|---|--|
| ☐ | ☐ | Recommend within category? |
| ☐ | ☐ | Recommend overall? |
| ☐ | ☐ | Interesting? |
| ☐ | ☐ | Unusual? |

THIS WHISKEY:
☐ Met expectations
☐ Exceeded expectations
☐ Disappointed

MY SCORE

1 to 10

IN A SINGLE WORD

# TASTING NOTES

| DATE | |
|------|--|
| LOCATION | |

**WHISKEY** [                    ]

DISTILLERY (*if known*)          PROOF          TYPE

PRICE          AGE STATEMENT (*if any*)          COLOR

## NOTES

*Check any that apply:*

☐ FLORAL  ☐ SPICY
☐ WOODY  ☐ SMOKY
☐ LEATHER  ☐ FRUITY
☐ CITRUS  ☐ SOLVENT/ASTRINGENT
☐ GRASS  ☐ HONEY/CARAMEL

*Mark on the spectrum:*

SWEET ← 10 8 6 4 2 0 2 4 6 8 10 → DRY

DELICATE ← 10 8 6 4 2 0 2 4 6 8 10 → BOLD

SMOOTH ← 10 8 6 4 2 0 2 4 6 8 10 → INTENSE

## OBSERVATIONS

_____

_____

_____

_____

_____

_____

## EVALUATION

| Y | N | |
|---|---|--|
| ☐ | ☐ | Recommend within category? |
| ☐ | ☐ | Recommend overall? |
| ☐ | ☐ | Interesting? |
| ☐ | ☐ | Unusual? |

THIS WHISKEY:
☐ Met expectations
☐ Exceeded expectations
☐ Disappointed

MY SCORE

[     ]

1 to 10

_____

IN A SINGLE WORD

# TASTING NOTES

| DATE | |
|------|--|
| LOCATION | |

**WHISKEY**

DISTILLERY (*if known*)          PROOF          TYPE

PRICE          AGE STATEMENT (*if any*)          COLOR

## NOTES

*Check any that apply:*

☐ FLORAL    ☐ SPICY
☐ WOODY    ☐ SMOKY
☐ LEATHER    ☐ FRUITY
☐ CITRUS    ☐ SOLVENT/ASTRINGENT
☐ GRASS    ☐ HONEY/CARAMEL

*Mark on the spectrum:*

SWEET                                             DRY
←—+—+—+—+—+—+—+—+—+—+—→
10  8   6   4   2   0   2   4   6   8  10

DELICATE                                        BOLD
←—+—+—+—+—+—+—+—+—+—+—→
10  8   6   4   2   0   2   4   6   8  10

SMOOTH                                       INTENSE
←—+—+—+—+—+—+—+—+—+—+—→
10  8   6   4   2   0   2   4   6   8  10

## OBSERVATIONS

_____

_____

_____

_____

_____

_____

## EVALUATION

| Y | N | |
|---|---|--|
| ☐ | ☐ | Recommend within category? |
| ☐ | ☐ | Recommend overall? |
| ☐ | ☐ | Interesting? |
| ☐ | ☐ | Unusual? |

THIS WHISKEY:
☐ Met expectations
☐ Exceeded expectations
☐ Disappointed

MY SCORE

[   ]

1 to 10

_____

IN A SINGLE WORD

# TASTING NOTES

| DATE | | WHISKEY | |
|------|--|---------|--|
| LOCATION | | | |

DISTILLERY (*if known*)    PROOF    TYPE

PRICE    AGE STATEMENT (*if any*)    COLOR

## NOTES

*Check any that apply:*

☐ FLORAL    ☐ SPICY

☐ WOODY    ☐ SMOKY

☐ LEATHER    ☐ FRUITY

☐ CITRUS    ☐ SOLVENT/ASTRINGENT

☐ GRASS    ☐ HONEY/CARAMEL

*Mark on the spectrum:*

SWEET    DRY
←|—|—|—|—|—|—|—|—|—|—|→
10  8  6  4  2  0  2  4  6  8  10

DELICATE    BOLD
←|—|—|—|—|—|—|—|—|—|—|→
10  8  6  4  2  0  2  4  6  8  10

SMOOTH    INTENSE
←|—|—|—|—|—|—|—|—|—|—|→
10  8  6  4  2  0  2  4  6  8  10

## OBSERVATIONS

_____

_____

_____

_____

_____

_____

## EVALUATION

| Y | N | | THIS WHISKEY: | MY SCORE |
|---|---|--|---------------|----------|
| ☐ | ☐ | Recommend within category? | ☐ Met expectations | |
| ☐ | ☐ | Recommend overall? | ☐ Exceeded expectations | |
| ☐ | ☐ | Interesting? | ☐ Disappointed | |
| ☐ | ☐ | Unusual? | | 1 to 10 |

IN A SINGLE WORD

# TASTING NOTES

| DATE | |
|---|---|
| LOCATION | |

**WHISKEY**

DISTILLERY (*if known*)　　　　PROOF　　　　TYPE

PRICE　　　　AGE STATEMENT (*if any*)　　　　COLOR

## NOTES

*Check any that apply:*

☐ FLORAL　☐ SPICY

☐ WOODY　☐ SMOKY

☐ LEATHER　☐ FRUITY

☐ CITRUS　☐ SOLVENT/ASTRINGENT

☐ GRASS　☐ HONEY/CARAMEL

*Mark on the spectrum:*

SWEET　　　　　　　　　　　　　　DRY

← | | | | | | | | | →
10　8　6　4　2　0　2　4　6　8　10

DELICATE　　　　　　　　　　　　BOLD

← | | | | | | | | | →
10　8　6　4　2　0　2　4　6　8　10

SMOOTH　　　　　　　　　　　INTENSE

← | | | | | | | | | →
10　8　6　4　2　0　2　4　6　8　10

## OBSERVATIONS

## EVALUATION

| Y | N | | |
|---|---|---|---|
| ☐ | ☐ | Recommend within category? |
| ☐ | ☐ | Recommend overall? |
| ☐ | ☐ | Interesting? |
| ☐ | ☐ | Unusual? |

THIS WHISKEY:

☐ Met expectations

☐ Exceeded expectations

☐ Disappointed

MY SCORE

1 to 10

IN A SINGLE WORD

# TASTING NOTES

| DATE | |
|---|---|
| LOCATION | |

**WHISKEY** [                    ]

DISTILLERY (*if known*)      PROOF      TYPE

PRICE      AGE STATEMENT (*if any*)      COLOR

## NOTES

*Check any that apply:*

- ☐ FLORAL
- ☐ WOODY
- ☐ LEATHER
- ☐ CITRUS
- ☐ GRASS
- ☐ SPICY
- ☐ SMOKY
- ☐ FRUITY
- ☐ SOLVENT/ASTRINGENT
- ☐ HONEY/CARAMEL

*Mark on the spectrum:*

SWEET                    DRY
← | | | | | | | | | →
10  8  6  4  2  0  2  4  6  8  10

DELICATE              BOLD
← | | | | | | | | | →
10  8  6  4  2  0  2  4  6  8  10

SMOOTH              INTENSE
← | | | | | | | | | →
10  8  6  4  2  0  2  4  6  8  10

## OBSERVATIONS

_____

_____

_____

_____

_____

_____

## EVALUATION

| Y | N | |
|---|---|---|
| ☐ | ☐ | Recommend within category? |
| ☐ | ☐ | Recommend overall? |
| ☐ | ☐ | Interesting? |
| ☐ | ☐ | Unusual? |

THIS WHISKEY:
- ☐ Met expectations
- ☐ Exceeded expectations
- ☐ Disappointed

MY SCORE

[        ]

1 to 10

_____

IN A SINGLE WORD

# TASTING NOTES

| DATE | |
|------|--|
| LOCATION | |

**WHISKEY**

DISTILLERY (*if known*)          PROOF          TYPE

PRICE          AGE STATEMENT (*if any*)          COLOR

## NOTES

*Check any that apply:*

☐ FLORAL    ☐ SPICY
☐ WOODY    ☐ SMOKY
☐ LEATHER    ☐ FRUITY
☐ CITRUS    ☐ SOLVENT/ASTRINGENT
☐ GRASS    ☐ HONEY/CARAMEL

*Mark on the spectrum:*

SWEET                                    DRY
←—+—+—+—+—+—+—+—+—+—→
10  8   6   4   2   0   2   4   6   8   10

DELICATE                              BOLD
←—+—+—+—+—+—+—+—+—+—→
10  8   6   4   2   0   2   4   6   8   10

SMOOTH                            INTENSE
←—+—+—+—+—+—+—+—+—+—→
10  8   6   4   2   0   2   4   6   8   10

## OBSERVATIONS

_____

_____

_____

_____

_____

_____

## EVALUATION

| Y | N | |
|---|---|--|
| ☐ | ☐ | Recommend within category? |
| ☐ | ☐ | Recommend overall? |
| ☐ | ☐ | Interesting? |
| ☐ | ☐ | Unusual? |

THIS WHISKEY:
☐ Met expectations
☐ Exceeded expectations
☐ Disappointed

MY SCORE

1 to 10

IN A SINGLE WORD

# TASTING NOTES

| DATE | | WHISKEY | |
| --- | --- | --- | --- |
| LOCATION | | | |

DISTILLERY (*if known*)  PROOF  TYPE

PRICE  AGE STATEMENT (*if any*)  COLOR

## NOTES

*Check any that apply:*

☐ FLORAL  ☐ SPICY
☐ WOODY  ☐ SMOKY
☐ LEATHER  ☐ FRUITY
☐ CITRUS  ☐ SOLVENT/ASTRINGENT
☐ GRASS  ☐ HONEY/CARAMEL

*Mark on the spectrum:*

SWEET  DRY
← + + + + + + + + + + →
10  8  6  4  2  0  2  4  6  8  10

DELICATE  BOLD
← + + + + + + + + + + →
10  8  6  4  2  0  2  4  6  8  10

SMOOTH  INTENSE
← + + + + + + + + + + →
10  8  6  4  2  0  2  4  6  8  10

## OBSERVATIONS

## EVALUATION

| Y | N | | THIS WHISKEY: | MY SCORE |
| --- | --- | --- | --- | --- |
| ☐ | ☐ | Recommend within category? | ☐ Met expectations | |
| ☐ | ☐ | Recommend overall? | ☐ Exceeded expectations | |
| ☐ | ☐ | Interesting? | ☐ Disappointed | |
| ☐ | ☐ | Unusual? | | 1 to 10 |

IN A SINGLE WORD

# TASTING NOTES

| DATE | |
|------|---|
| LOCATION | |

WHISKEY

DISTILLERY (*if known*)      PROOF      TYPE

PRICE      AGE STATEMENT (*if any*)      COLOR

## NOTES

*Check any that apply:*

- ☐ FLORAL
- ☐ WOODY
- ☐ LEATHER
- ☐ CITRUS
- ☐ GRASS

- ☐ SPICY
- ☐ SMOKY
- ☐ FRUITY
- ☐ SOLVENT/ASTRINGENT
- ☐ HONEY/CARAMEL

*Mark on the spectrum:*

SWEET ⟵———————————⟶ DRY
10  8  6  4  2  0  2  4  6  8  10

DELICATE ⟵———————————⟶ BOLD
10  8  6  4  2  0  2  4  6  8  10

SMOOTH ⟵———————————⟶ INTENSE
10  8  6  4  2  0  2  4  6  8  10

## OBSERVATIONS

_____

_____

_____

_____

_____

_____

## EVALUATION

| Y | N | |
|---|---|---|
| ☐ | ☐ | Recommend within category? |
| ☐ | ☐ | Recommend overall? |
| ☐ | ☐ | Interesting? |
| ☐ | ☐ | Unusual? |

THIS WHISKEY:
- ☐ Met expectations
- ☐ Exceeded expectations
- ☐ Disappointed

MY SCORE

1 to 10

IN A SINGLE WORD

# TASTING NOTES

| DATE | |
|---|---|
| LOCATION | |

**WHISKEY**

DISTILLERY (*if known*)    PROOF    TYPE

PRICE    AGE STATEMENT (*if any*)    COLOR

## NOTES

*Check any that apply:*

- ☐ FLORAL      ☐ SPICY
- ☐ WOODY       ☐ SMOKY
- ☐ LEATHER     ☐ FRUITY
- ☐ CITRUS      ☐ SOLVENT/ASTRINGENT
- ☐ GRASS       ☐ HONEY/CARAMEL

*Mark on the spectrum:*

SWEET ←|—|—|—|—|—|—|—|—|—|→ DRY
10  8  6  4  2  0  2  4  6  8  10

DELICATE ←|—|—|—|—|—|—|—|—|—|→ BOLD
10  8  6  4  2  0  2  4  6  8  10

SMOOTH ←|—|—|—|—|—|—|—|—|—|→ INTENSE
10  8  6  4  2  0  2  4  6  8  10

## OBSERVATIONS

_____
_____
_____
_____
_____
_____

## EVALUATION

| Y | N | | |
|---|---|---|---|
| ☐ | ☐ | Recommend within category? |
| ☐ | ☐ | Recommend overall? |
| ☐ | ☐ | Interesting? |
| ☐ | ☐ | Unusual? |

THIS WHISKEY:
- ☐ Met expectations
- ☐ Exceeded expectations
- ☐ Disappointed

MY SCORE

☐

1 to 10

IN A SINGLE WORD

# TASTING NOTES

| DATE | |
|------|---|
| LOCATION | |

**WHISKEY**

DISTILLERY (*if known*)    PROOF    TYPE

PRICE    AGE STATEMENT (*if any*)    COLOR

## NOTES

*Check any that apply:*

☐ FLORAL    ☐ SPICY
☐ WOODY    ☐ SMOKY
☐ LEATHER    ☐ FRUITY
☐ CITRUS    ☐ SOLVENT/ASTRINGENT
☐ GRASS    ☐ HONEY/CARAMEL

*Mark on the spectrum:*

SWEET                                          DRY
← | | | | | | | | | | →
10  8  6  4  2  0  2  4  6  8  10

DELICATE                                      BOLD
← | | | | | | | | | | →
10  8  6  4  2  0  2  4  6  8  10

SMOOTH                                    INTENSE
← | | | | | | | | | | →
10  8  6  4  2  0  2  4  6  8  10

## OBSERVATIONS

## EVALUATION

| Y | N | | |
|---|---|---|---|
| ☐ | ☐ | Recommend within category? | |
| ☐ | ☐ | Recommend overall? | |
| ☐ | ☐ | Interesting? | |
| ☐ | ☐ | Unusual? | |

THIS WHISKEY:
☐ Met expectations
☐ Exceeded expectations
☐ Disappointed

MY SCORE

1 to 10

IN A SINGLE WORD

# TASTING NOTES

| DATE | |
|------|--|
| LOCATION | |

**WHISKEY**

DISTILLERY (*if known*)  PROOF  TYPE

PRICE  AGE STATEMENT (*if any*)  COLOR

## NOTES

*Check any that apply:*

☐ FLORAL  ☐ SPICY

☐ WOODY  ☐ SMOKY

☐ LEATHER  ☐ FRUITY

☐ CITRUS  ☐ SOLVENT/ASTRINGENT

☐ GRASS  ☐ HONEY/CARAMEL

*Mark on the spectrum:*

SWEET  DRY

10  8  6  4  2  0  2  4  6  8  10

DELICATE  BOLD

10  8  6  4  2  0  2  4  6  8  10

SMOOTH  INTENSE

10  8  6  4  2  0  2  4  6  8  10

## OBSERVATIONS

## EVALUATION

| Y | N | | THIS WHISKEY: | MY SCORE |
|---|---|--|---------------|----------|
| ☐ | ☐ | Recommend within category? | ☐ Met expectations | |
| ☐ | ☐ | Recommend overall? | ☐ Exceeded expectations | |
| ☐ | ☐ | Interesting? | ☐ Disappointed | |
| ☐ | ☐ | Unusual? | | 1 to 10 |

IN A SINGLE WORD

# TASTING NOTES

| DATE | |
|---|---|
| LOCATION | |

**WHISKEY**

---

DISTILLERY (*if known*)  PROOF  TYPE

---

PRICE  AGE STATEMENT (*if any*)  COLOR

## NOTES

*Check any that apply:*

☐ FLORAL  ☐ SPICY
☐ WOODY  ☐ SMOKY
☐ LEATHER  ☐ FRUITY
☐ CITRUS  ☐ SOLVENT/ASTRINGENT
☐ GRASS  ☐ HONEY/CARAMEL

*Mark on the spectrum:*

SWEET  DRY
←—+—+—+—+—+—+—+—+—+—→
10  8  6  4  2  0  2  4  6  8  10

DELICATE  BOLD
←—+—+—+—+—+—+—+—+—+—→
10  8  6  4  2  0  2  4  6  8  10

SMOOTH  INTENSE
←—+—+—+—+—+—+—+—+—+—→
10  8  6  4  2  0  2  4  6  8  10

## OBSERVATIONS

_____

_____

_____

_____

_____

_____

## EVALUATION

| Y | N | | THIS WHISKEY: | MY SCORE |
|---|---|---|---|---|
| ☐ | ☐ | Recommend within category? | ☐ Met expectations | |
| ☐ | ☐ | Recommend overall? | ☐ Exceeded expectations | |
| ☐ | ☐ | Interesting? | ☐ Disappointed | |
| ☐ | ☐ | Unusual? | | 1 to 10 |

IN A SINGLE WORD

# TASTING NOTES

| DATE | | |
|---|---|---|
| LOCATION | | |

**WHISKEY**

DISTILLERY (*if known*)          PROOF          TYPE

PRICE          AGE STATEMENT (*if any*)          COLOR

## NOTES

*Check any that apply:*

- ☐ FLORAL   ☐ SPICY
- ☐ WOODY   ☐ SMOKY
- ☐ LEATHER   ☐ FRUITY
- ☐ CITRUS   ☐ SOLVENT/ASTRINGENT
- ☐ GRASS   ☐ HONEY/CARAMEL

*Mark on the spectrum:*

SWEET                                           DRY
←—+——+——+——+——+——+——+——+——+——+——→
10   8   6   4   2   0   2   4   6   8   10

DELICATE                                        BOLD
←—+——+——+——+——+——+——+——+——+——+——→
10   8   6   4   2   0   2   4   6   8   10

SMOOTH                                     INTENSE
←—+——+——+——+——+——+——+——+——+——+——→
10   8   6   4   2   0   2   4   6   8   10

## OBSERVATIONS

_____

_____

_____

_____

_____

_____

## EVALUATION

| Y | N | | THIS WHISKEY: | MY SCORE |
|---|---|---|---|---|
| ☐ | ☐ | Recommend within category? | ☐ Met expectations | |
| ☐ | ☐ | Recommend overall? | ☐ Exceeded expectations | |
| ☐ | ☐ | Interesting? | ☐ Disappointed | |
| ☐ | ☐ | Unusual? | | 1 to 10 |

_____

IN A SINGLE WORD

# TASTING NOTES

| DATE | | | |
|---|---|---|---|
| LOCATION | | | |

**WHISKEY** _____

DISTILLERY (*if known*)      PROOF      TYPE

PRICE      AGE STATEMENT (*if any*)      COLOR

## NOTES

*Check any that apply:*

☐ FLORAL    ☐ SPICY
☐ WOODY    ☐ SMOKY
☐ LEATHER    ☐ FRUITY
☐ CITRUS    ☐ SOLVENT/ASTRINGENT
☐ GRASS    ☐ HONEY/CARAMEL

*Mark on the spectrum:*

SWEET          DRY
← + + + + + + + + + →
10   8   6   4   2   0   2   4   6   8   10

DELICATE          BOLD
← + + + + + + + + + →
10   8   6   4   2   0   2   4   6   8   10

SMOOTH          INTENSE
← + + + + + + + + + →
10   8   6   4   2   0   2   4   6   8   10

## OBSERVATIONS

_____

_____

_____

_____

_____

_____

## EVALUATION

| Y | N | |
|---|---|---|
| ☐ | ☐ | Recommend within category? |
| ☐ | ☐ | Recommend overall? |
| ☐ | ☐ | Interesting? |
| ☐ | ☐ | Unusual? |

THIS WHISKEY:
☐ Met expectations
☐ Exceeded expectations
☐ Disappointed

MY SCORE

[     ]

1 to 10

_____

IN A SINGLE WORD

# TASTING NOTES

| DATE | |
|------|--|
| LOCATION | |

**WHISKEY**

DISTILLERY (*if known*)          PROOF          TYPE

PRICE          AGE STATEMENT (*if any*)          COLOR

## NOTES

*Check any that apply:*

☐ FLORAL   ☐ SPICY
☐ WOODY   ☐ SMOKY
☐ LEATHER   ☐ FRUITY
☐ CITRUS   ☐ SOLVENT/ASTRINGENT
☐ GRASS   ☐ HONEY/CARAMEL

*Mark on the spectrum:*

SWEET                                         DRY
←—+—+—+—+—+—+—+—+—+—→
10  8   6   4   2   0   2   4   6   8   10

DELICATE                                      BOLD
←—+—+—+—+—+—+—+—+—+—→
10  8   6   4   2   0   2   4   6   8   10

SMOOTH                                    INTENSE
←—+—+—+—+—+—+—+—+—+—→
10  8   6   4   2   0   2   4   6   8   10

## OBSERVATIONS

_____

_____

_____

_____

_____

_____

## EVALUATION

| Y | N | |
|---|---|--|
| ☐ | ☐ | Recommend within category? |
| ☐ | ☐ | Recommend overall? |
| ☐ | ☐ | Interesting? |
| ☐ | ☐ | Unusual? |

THIS WHISKEY:
☐ Met expectations
☐ Exceeded expectations
☐ Disappointed

MY SCORE

[   ]

1 to 10

_____

IN A SINGLE WORD

# TASTING NOTES

| | |
|---|---|
| DATE | |
| LOCATION | |

**WHISKEY**

DISTILLERY (*if known*)      PROOF      TYPE

PRICE      AGE STATEMENT (*if any*)      COLOR

## NOTES

*Check any that apply:*

- ☐ FLORAL
- ☐ WOODY
- ☐ LEATHER
- ☐ CITRUS
- ☐ GRASS

- ☐ SPICY
- ☐ SMOKY
- ☐ FRUITY
- ☐ SOLVENT/ASTRINGENT
- ☐ HONEY/CARAMEL

*Mark on the spectrum:*

SWEET            DRY

←———+———+———+———+———+———+———+———+———+———→
10  8  6  4  2  0  2  4  6  8  10

DELICATE            BOLD

←———+———+———+———+———+———+———+———+———+———→
10  8  6  4  2  0  2  4  6  8  10

SMOOTH            INTENSE

←———+———+———+———+———+———+———+———+———+———→
10  8  6  4  2  0  2  4  6  8  10

## OBSERVATIONS

_____

_____

_____

_____

_____

_____

## EVALUATION

| Y | N | |
|---|---|---|
| ☐ | ☐ | Recommend within category? |
| ☐ | ☐ | Recommend overall? |
| ☐ | ☐ | Interesting? |
| ☐ | ☐ | Unusual? |

THIS WHISKEY:
- ☐ Met expectations
- ☐ Exceeded expectations
- ☐ Disappointed

MY SCORE

[ ]

1 to 10

IN A SINGLE WORD

# TASTING NOTES

| DATE | | WHISKEY | |
| --- | --- | --- | --- |
| LOCATION | | | |

DISTILLERY (if known)  PROOF  TYPE

PRICE  AGE STATEMENT (if any)  COLOR

## NOTES

*Check any that apply:*

☐ FLORAL  ☐ SPICY

☐ WOODY  ☐ SMOKY

☐ LEATHER  ☐ FRUITY

☐ CITRUS  ☐ SOLVENT/ASTRINGENT

☐ GRASS  ☐ HONEY/CARAMEL

*Mark on the spectrum:*

SWEET  DRY

←—+—+—+—+—+—+—+—+—+—→

10  8  6  4  2  0  2  4  6  8  10

DELICATE  BOLD

←—+—+—+—+—+—+—+—+—+—→

10  8  6  4  2  0  2  4  6  8  10

SMOOTH  INTENSE

←—+—+—+—+—+—+—+—+—+—→

10  8  6  4  2  0  2  4  6  8  10

## OBSERVATIONS

## EVALUATION

| Y | N | | THIS WHISKEY: | MY SCORE |
| --- | --- | --- | --- | --- |
| ☐ | ☐ | Recommend within category? | ☐ Met expectations | |
| ☐ | ☐ | Recommend overall? | ☐ Exceeded expectations | |
| ☐ | ☐ | Interesting? | ☐ Disappointed | |
| ☐ | ☐ | Unusual? | | 1 to 10 |

IN A SINGLE WORD

**DESIGNER:** Danielle Deschenes
**ISBN:** 978-1-4197-1576-1

Printed in China
10  9  8  7  6  5  4  3

*Abrams Noterie products are available at special discounts when
purchased in quantity for premiums and promotions as well as
fundraising or educational use. Special editions can also be created
to specification. For details, contact specialsales@abramsbooks.com
or the address below.*

THE ART OF BOOKS SINCE 1949
115 West 18th Street
New York, NY 10011
www.abramsbooks.com